VIA Folios 61

The Poet's Cookbook

The Poet's Cookbook

Recipes from Tuscany by

GRACE CAVALIERI & SABINE PASCARELLI

Poems by

28 ITALIAN & AMERICAN POETS

Traduzione di

SABINE PASCARELLI

BORDIGHERA PRESS

Library of Congress Control Number: 2009908619

Cover photograph by Dan Murano

© 2009 by Grace Cavalieri & Sabine Pascarelli

Printed in the United States.

Published by
BORDIGHERA PRESS
John D. Calandra Italian American Institute
25 W. 43rd Street, 17th Floor
New York, NY 10036

VIA FOLIOS 61
ISBN 978–1–59954–011–5

Sabine gives gratitude and thanks to her friend Noreen Flocchini for valuable and illuminating advice during the translation process. Sabine also gives heartfelt thanks to her poet friend Gabriella Gianfelici, and her husband Salvatore for their expert counsel. Grace wants to acknowledge her husband Kenneth Flynn and talented friend Pamela Mann whose good will and helping hands made the process possible.

Sabine è grata alla sua amica Noreen Flocchini per la sua preziosa ed illuminante consulenza durante il processo della traduzione. Sabine ringrazia di cuore anche la sua amica poeta Gabriella Gianfelici e il suo marito Salvatore per i loro competenti consigli. Grace è riconoscente a suo marito Kenneth Flynn e alla esperta amica Pamela Mann che hanno reso possibile tutto ciò con la loro abilità e molto impegno.

Grace Cavalieri dedicates this book to Angelo Cavalieri

Sabine Pascarelli dedicates this book to Salvatore Pascarelli

THE POET'S COOKBOOK
Introduction by Grace Cavalieri

There are many standard national cookbooks in English and Italian. However, Sabine Pascarelli and I want to share recipes that were once purely Italian and are now becoming Italo-American. Sabine lives in Tuscany, the birthplace of my parents. Our lineage is the same, and our kitchens are very much the same, although one home overlooks an olive grove near Florence, and the other is near the sailboats of Annapolis. Because we came to our friendship through poetry and cooking, we offer some of each in this book. Cooking speaks of community, in Italy and America; and the breaking of bread in any language, in every country, speaks of a commonality with friends. In this spirit, although the recipes are our own, we asked that the poems included be from our friends, other poets.

Regional cooking has its own style and its own season. It also has a time-honored history, especially in Italy. The first kitchens that celebrated natural foods, seasonal herbs, thoughtful cooking and a consciousness of health were in the monasteries. During Medieval times, these first true kitchens welcomed travelers into a cultural sanctuary that provided both physical and intellectual nourishment. The monks cultivated their own gardens and from simple resources provided recipes that through the ages have been embellished, enhanced and adorned. But the basic idea of wholesome cooking was born in a place of worship. This impresses us greatly, because the study of herbs and the benefits of food are proven and fully acknowledged all these years later. The benefits of nutrition through delicious cooking now fortify the original studies of the Italian agrarians. For instance, we believe that herbs, sage, basil, rosemary, thyme, easily grown in our own backyards, or found in a nearby market, add a wealth and richness to every kitchen. Now food scientists are proving herbs to be among the most beneficial of all ingredients. From the earliest traditions of Italy, we take the wisdom of our ancestors and create modern day menus. Everyone is busy and productive in today's society. These recipes are for the person who has a love of excellent dining and yet has only a minimal time to cook. Sabine Pascarelli and Grace Cavalieri cook in a modern moment. However the cuisine, now thought to be gourmet fare, is very much part of a long awakening from ancient origins.

Because we are writers, and share a love of poetry, we are honored and proud to present additional nourishment, 28 poets, each serving up a delicious poem.

Grace Cavalieri   Sabine Pascarelli

TABLE OF CONTENTS

APPETIZERS — ANTIPASTI

Mozzarella in a Carriage — Mozzarella in Carrozza
Fried Mozzarella — Mozzarelline Fritte
Stuffed Tomatoes — Pomodori Saporiti
Italian Antipasto — Antipasto Misto
Prosciutto with Cantaloupe — Prosciutto e Melone
Olive Pâté — Pâté di Olive
Bruschetta with Tomato and Basil — Bruschetta al Pomodoro
Chick-Peas in Garlic Oil — Ceci all'Olio
Italian Mushroom Relish — Funghi sotto Olio
Eggplant Antipasto — Caponata

Mozzarella in a Carriage — Mozzarella in Carrozza

8 Slices of thick bread
3 eggs, to beat together with
  2 T milk;
Butter or olive oil for frying

mozzarella ball (with one ball
  you will make 4 slices)
Salt and ground pepper for
  seasoning

Cut off crust of bread and cut slices in halves. Place a thin slice of mozzarella on each of 8 half slices of bread and cover with the other half slices to make 16 half sandwiches. Dip bread (with cheese inside) in milk. Heat butter in frying pan and fry sandwiches on both sides until golden brown. Serve immediately. Very good as appetizers. Serves 2–4.

Fried Mozzarella — Mozzarelline Fritte

¾ pound mozzarella
2 eggs, lightly beaten with
cup bread crumbs

½ cup flour
¼ tsp salt
1 cup olive oil

Cut mozzarella into 4-inch squares, 2 inches thick. Roll in flour, dip into egg, roll in bread crumbs, again into egg and again into bread crumbs. Fry in hot oil just long enough for the bread crumbs to turn golden in color. Serve immediately. Serves 4.

Stuffed Tomatoes — Pomodori Saporiti

4 large firm tomatoes
2 hard boiled eggs, diced fine
1 small can tuna fish, grated
¼ t pepper

1 t capers
1 t chopped parsley
2 T mayonnaise

Cut tops off tomatoes and remove seeds and liquid. Mix together eggs, tuna, pepper, capers, parsley and mayonnaise. Fill tomatoes with mixture, chill and serve. Serves 4.

Italian Antipasto — Antipasto Misto

4 thin slices Italian Salami
4 thin slices prosciutto
4 anchovy filets
2 celery hearts, cut in
 halves, lengthwise
1 small can Italian tuna fish
1 small can imported Italian antipasto
    (optional)

8 large green olives
2 t capers
4 artichoke hearts in oil
1 small can pimentos
4 slices tomato
4 vinegar peppers
8 black ripe olives

Use a large oval platter. Place tuna fish and imported antipasto in center of dish and arrange all the other ingredients around, making as pretty a pattern as you can. Serve with crusty Italian bread and butter. Serves 4.

Prosciutto with Cantaloupe — Prosciutto e Melone

Tuscan prosciutto is more salted than the more widely known variety, and perfect for sweet cantaloupes, Tuscan prosciutto also pairs well with fresh green or purple figs.

1 cantaloupe, seeded and cut into 8 wedges
16 paper-thin slices Tuscan prosciutto

Place 2 cantaloupe wedges on each plate. Arrange 4 prosciutto slices alongside the cantaloupe or drape it over it. Serve immediately.

Olive Pâté — Pâté di Olive

1 can black olives (pitted)   2 t capers
4 anchovy filets   4 teaspoons mustard
2 cloves garlic   fresh ground pepper

In a plastic bowl, blend the olives with the other ingredients until the mixture is creamy and spreadable. Toast the bread on both sides, rub each slice with garlic. Spread the bread with olive pâté. Serve at room temperature. It keeps for almost a couple of weeks in the refrigerator, best in small closed container.

Bruschetta with Tomato and Basil — Bruschetta al Pomodoro

8 bread slices
4 large ripe tomatoes
(or 8 ripe plum tomatoes), diced
Salt, pepper

4 garlic cloves
1 sprig of basil
Extra-virgin Olive oil

Put in a container the tomatoes, add salt, pepper, olive oil and basil. Let it marinate for at least 30 minutes, better more. Meanwhile, toast the slices of bread on both sides under the broiler. Rub them with garlic while they are still hot and put back under the broiler for a moment, then season with the marinated tomato sauce previously prepared.

Chick-Peas in Garlic Oil — Ceci all'Olio

1 can chick-peas
½ t freshly ground black pepper
1 t salt

¼ cup olive oil
2 t lemon juice
1 T minced parsley

Drain the chick-peas very thoroughly. Heat the oil in a skillet; add the garlic and chick-peas. Sauté until lightly browned. Drain well. Season with the salt, pepper, lemon juice, and parsley. Blend to use as spread. Serve hot or cold. Serves 4–6.

Italian Mushroom Relish — Funghi sotto Olio

¼ cup olive oil
1 cup chopped onions
¾ cup diced celery
¾ cup chopped tomatoes
⅛ t oregano

1 pound button or sliced
   mushrooms
½ t salt
¼ t black pepper
1 T lemon juice

Heat the oil in a saucepan; sauté the onions and celery 5 minutes. Add the tomatoes and lemon juice; cook over low heat 15 minutes. Add the mushrooms, salt, pepper and oregano; cook 10 minutes. Cool, then chill. The mushrooms keep for about 1 week. Makes about 2 cups.

Eggplant Antipasto — Caponata

1 large eggplant
1 ½ cups diced onions
1 16-ounce can tomatoes,
   chopped
2 t sugar
½ cup diced black olives
1 T pine nuts or sliced almonds

⅔ cup olive oil
1 cup diced celery
1 t salt
¼ t freshly ground black
   pepper
2 T capers

Peel the eggplant and cut into 1-inch cubes. Heat half the oil in a skillet; sauté the eggplant until browned. Remove. Add the remaining oil to the skillet; sauté the onions 10 minutes. Add the celery and tomatoes; cook over low heat 20 minutes.

Bring to a boil the vinegar, salt, pepper and sugar; add to the skillet with the olives, capers, nuts, sautéed eggplant. Cover and cook over low heat 20 minutes; stir frequently to prevent sticking. Taste for seasoning. Cool, then chill. Caponata keeps in the refrigerator for about 2 weeks. Serve with Italian or French bread as a first course or hors d'oeuvre. Makes about 4 cups.

Sunday at Nonna's

Walking through Nonna's iron-latticed door
in Bensonhurst on any given Sunday,
we were enveloped by the savory
odors of freshly-stuffed sausage,
onions and garlic, sizzling in a pan,
the licorice scent of fennel
hand-picked from her yard.
We would find her, still in black,

though widowed some twenty years earlier,
her apron caked with grease and marinara,
dispensing anisette cookies to the youngest cousins
all the while putting her tongue on the roof
of her mouth behind her front teeth, hissing
whenever anything displeased her.
That sound sent chills up our spines, young
and old alike, and we knew never to complain

about the plastic shrouding the furniture,
the gargantuan crucifix looming above
the dining room table. Not to complain. Period.
But once the sumptuous pasta tumbled onto plates
and forks were lifted, their silver glinting
like Vatican treasures, we all laughed, paused, and raised
our glasses in a toast to Nonna, the matriarch, the arbiter
of order, the feared, the beloved, the keeper of the feast.

— *Calder Lowe*

Domenica da Nonna

Entrando dal cancello di Nonna
a Bensenhurst ogni domenica che fu,
venivamo avvolti da gustosi
odori di salsiccia appena cotta,
cipolle ed aglio, rosolando in una padella,
il profumo di finocchio, come liquirizia,
raccolto a mano dal suo giardino.
La trovavamo, ancora in nero,

vedova ormai da più di vent'anni,
il grembiule incrostato di unto e sugo di pomodoro,
a distribuire biscotti di anice ai cugini più piccoli,
mentre teneva la lingua sul palato
dietro ai denti, sibilando
ogni volta che qualcosa la contrariava.
Quel suono mandava brividi lungo la schiena,
a piccoli e grandi, e non ci saremmo mai lamentati

della plastica, che avvolgeva i mobili,
del gigantesco crocifisso incombente sul
tavolo della sala da pranzo. Non lamentarsi. Punto.
Ma non appena la sontuosa pasta ruzzolò nei piatti
e le forchette si alzarono, scintillanti d'argento
come i tesori del Vaticano, tutti noi ridevamo, ci fermavamo
alzando i bicchieri per un brindisi a Nonna, la matriarca, l'arbitro
dell'ordine, la temuta, l'amata, la custode della festa.

— *Calder Lowe*
trans: *Sabine Pascarelli*

Tomatoes in September

Every surface in the house covered
         with tomatoes, a vat
of boiling water on the stove,
         drop them in and wait to see

cracks in their skin, into cold water, out,
         cut away the bad spots,
cut out stem end and blossom end,
         peel away the skin,

chop them up, drain them in a colander,
         dump them into the other
pot in which a mountain of garlic
         has been simmering in olive oil:

Brandywine, Juliet, Cosmonaut,
         Rosa de Bern, all go in,
salt and pepper, then
         let them bubble

while you
         go smell the house.

— *David Budbill*

Pomodori a Settembre

Ogni superficie della casa coperta
      di pomodori, un pentolone
d'acqua bollente sul fuoco,
      immergili e aspetta di vedere

la buccia screpolata, giù in acqua fredda, fuori,
      togli le parti guaste,
taglia i finali di gambo e fiore,
      togli la buccia,

sminuzzali, falli scolare nel colapasta,
      gettali nell'altra
pentola, dove una montagna di aglio
      sfrigola in olio d'oliva

Brandywine, Juliet, Cosmonaut,
      Rosa de Bern, tutti dentro,
sale, pepe, e poi
      lascia bollire tutto

mentre tu
      vai ad annusare la casa.

— *David Budbill*
trans: *Sabine Pascarelli*

"He Was A Bold Man That First Ate An Oyster"

Spake the American Jonathan Swift and set the women of the
world to wondering what they would be if they swallowed
the oyster raw—cold, slimy, and full of zinc, a mineral
required for the production of testosterone.

Did this give rise to the maxim, "Eat Oysters, Love Longer?"
How about the baked oyster smothered Italian style in tomatoes,
olive oil, oregano, and garlic, garlic, garlic? Imagine an accompanying
label that proclaims: "This oyster has undergone at least one sex change
and incubated one million larvae."

Or now floating in Italian corn chowder with orzo, so mysterious,
so amorphous, possibly androgynous, also rich in iodine and low in
cholesterol, preparing the consumer for *innamoramento* or *amore vietato*.
No wonder the dashing Casanova started a meal by eating 12 dozen
oysters.

— *Ernie Wormwood*

Fu un Uomo Ardito a mangiare per Primo un'Ostrica

Disse l'americano Jonathan Swift e spinse le donne del
mondo a chiedersi che sarebbe di loro se ingoiassero
l'ostrica cruda—fredda, vischiosa e piena di zinco, minerale
integrante per la produzione di testosterone.

Era questo che fece nascere la massima "Mangia ostriche e amerai più
a lungo?"
E che dire delle ostriche cotte al forno, ricoperte all'italiana di pomodori,
olio d'oliva, origano e aglio, aglio, aglio? Immaginatele provviste di
etichetta
che dichiara: "Questa ostrica ha subito almeno un cambiamento di sesso
e ha incubato un milione di larve."

Oppure adesso, galleggiando in una zuppa italiana di mais ed orzo, così
misteriosa,
così amorfa, possibilmente androgena, in più ricca di iodio e povera di
colesterolo, sta preparando il consumatore per *innamoramento o amore
vietato*.
Non sorprende che l'irruente Casanova iniziò un pasto mangiando 12
dozzine di ostriche.

— *Ernie Wormwood*
trans: *Sabine Pascarelli*

Pears

Some say
it was a pear
Eve ate.
Why else the shape
of the womb,
or of the cello
whose single song is grief
for the parent tree?
Why else the fruit itself
tawny and sweet
which your lover
over breakfast
lets go your pear-
shaped breast
to reach for?

— *Linda Pastan*

Pere

Alcuni dicono
che era una pera
quella che Eva mangiò.
Altrimenti perché
la forma dell'utero
o del violoncello
la cui unica canzone è dolore
per l'albero d'origine?
Altrimenti, perché la frutta stessa
fulva e dolce
per cui il tuo amante
durante la prima colazione
lascia il tuo seno a
forma di pera,
allungando la mano?

— *Linda Pastan*
trans: *Sabine Pascarelli*

Soup

At 4 PM, while her ex is sitting
in his easy chair somewhere in the gray
of his Iowa landscape, his desk high

with obligations, the unread
Sunday papers piled by his feet,
the winds faint, the traffic fainter,

the snowless cold out every
window of his house, and light
thrown through the clouds in such a way

there is no doubt what time
or day or state this is,
a little farther south

she will be standing at the kitchen sink
of her too familiar house, scraping
vegetables for soup and looking

out at the same bleak sky, trying
to remember how brilliant
the brittle trees have been,

listening to their fits
and twists in the wind, paring
carrot peels into the sink, then potato,

letting them pile there like spent

Minestrone

Alle ore 16.00, mentre il suo ex è seduto
su una comoda sedia da qualche parte nel grigio
del suo paesaggio dell'Iowa, la scrivania piena

di obblighi, I giornali non letti
di domenica accumulati ai suoi piedi,
i venti lievi, il traffico più lieve ancora,

il freddo senza neve fuori da ogni
finestra della sua casa, e luce
che filtra dalle nuvole in una maniera

che non lascia dubbi in che ora,
giorno o Stato ci troviamo,
un po' più a sud

lei in piedi davanti al lavandino di cucina
della sua casa fin troppo familiare, sbucciando
verdure per la minestra e guardando

fuori lo stesso tetro cielo, cercando
di ricordare com'erano splendidi
i fragili alberi,

ascoltando I loro scricchiolii
e cigolii nel vento, pelando
bucce di carota nel lavandino, poi di patata,

lasciandole ammucchiare come pelle

snake skins. If only he
would open this door, how warm

the afternoon would feel, how different
the falling of the light, how autumn,
not winter, the soup.

— *Andrea Hollander Budy*

di serpente svuotata. Lui, se solo
aprisse questa porta, quanto più

caldo sarebbe questo pomeriggio, quanto
diversa la luce, quanto autunno,
non inverno, il minestrone.

— *Andrea Hollander Budy*
trans: *Sabine Pascarelli*

SOUPS — MINESTRE

Leek Soup — Crema di Porri
Tomato Soup with Bread — Pappa al Pomodoro
Stew — Zuppa "Stufata"
Onion Soup — Zuppa di Cipolle
Ceci Bean Soup — Terrina di Pasta e Ceci
Fish Soup — Zuppa di Pesce
Lentil Soup — Zuppa di Lenticchie
Zucchini Soup — Crema di Zucchine
Cucumber Soup — Crema di Cetrioli
Vegetable and Bread Soup — Ribollita

Leek Soup — Crema di Porri

2 leeks — clean well   2 onions
1 glass of white wine   2 t flour
1 cup stock   ½ cup of creamy cheese
2 cups of milk (or a cup of cream)   Parsley
4 t Parmesan   Salt

Finely chop the leeks into rings, with the chopped onion and fry a little butter in a pot or casserole dish until light golden. Add the flour and salt, and pour in stock, stirring all the time. Add the wine. Cook for about twenty minutes, remove from the heat and add the milk. To make the mixture creamy in consistency, melt the creamy cheese into the soup, you could put it into a blender for a minute or two. Return to the heat for five minutes, add the chopped parsley and grated Parmesan and serve immediately.

Tomato Soup with Bread — Pappa al Pomodoro

One onion	One leek	One carrot
One stick of celery	4 t extra-virgin	4 tomatoes
Sprig of fresh sage	olive oil	Basil
6 slices hard unsalted	Salt	Extra-virgin olive oil
bread	Fresh ground black pepper	

Finely chop the onion, leek, carrot, and celery and fry with the oil in a large pan. Add salt, the peeled and chopped tomatoes, sage and basil and cook over low heat. Add water until it becomes smooth and creamy, not too thick, not too liquid. The soup should be served tepid, with olive oil drizzled on top. The flavor can be heightened with a dash of pepper or red paprika.

The original recipe was without tomatoes, as it dates from long before the discovery of America and their arrival in Europe. The ingredients were therefore simply bread, oil, garlic and salt and this tasty, mushy mixture often was used to wean babies.

Stew — Zuppa "Stufata"

2 onions, chopped
1 pound beef meat, cut into cubes
2 T red paprika seasoning
2 cloves garlic
Cumin
Salt
Water to cover

4 large potatoes, cut into small
  cubes
2 carrots, chopped
3 large tomatoes
1 red or yellow pepper,
  chopped

Fry the onions in olive oil until golden. Add the meat cubes, 2 T of red paprika seasoning and the garlic cloves. Cover and let simmer for a while. Add cumin, salt, the carrots, tomatoes and pepper, and cover with water. When the meat is half cooked, add the potatoes, more water, and let it simmer all together until meat and potatoes are soft. Serves 4.

Onion Soup — Zuppa di Cipolle

4-5 large onions
5T butter
4T beefstock (paste)

3 quarts water or enough
  canned beef broth to cover
  onions

Sauté sliced onions in 4T butter over medium high heat until caramel. Boil water with stock or broth. Place onions in broth, bring back to boil. Cover and simmer for one hour. Sprinkle beef bullion granules for richness to taste. Serve with grated cheese and croutons. Serves 5. Vegetable bullion can replace beef, but more seasoning is then required.

Ceci Bean Soup — Terrina di Pasta e Ceci
(Ceci = chickpeas or garbanza beans)

⅓ cup diced pancetta or
    bacon or ham
1 yellow onion, chopped
1 fresh rosemary sprig
4 fresh sage leaves, chopped
2 large tomatoes, peeled
    seeded and chopped

3 cups cooked ceci beans
5 cups chicken broth
1 garlic clove, minced
Salt and freshly ground pepper,
    to taste
Extra Virgin olive oil for
    serving

In a soup pot over medium-low heat, fry the pancetta, stirring, until golden, 4 to 6 minutes. Add the onion and garlic and fry, stirring, until translucent, 4 to 6 minutes. Reduce the heat to low, add the sage and tomatoes and cook, stirring, until the tomatoes are tender, 6 to 8 minutes. Add the ceci beans, broth and rosemary and cook, stirring for 20 minutes.

Remove the rosemary and discard. Take out half of the ceci beans and blend them, until smooth, then give them back into the pot. Season with salt and pepper. Ladle the soup into individual bowls and drizzle with olive oil. Serves 4 to 6.

Fish Soup — Zuppa di Pesce

2 stalks celery
3 carrots
Handful spinach
Can diced tomatoes
Chicken, beef, or vegetable bullion

1 lb. frozen flounder
1 large onion
Any leftover vegetables, or
    beans, or barley, or rice

Cover vegetables in water. Generously sprinkle with chicken, beef or vegetable bullion. Add can of diced tomatoes, add parsley and garlic salt. Boil until vegetables are tender, about 20 minutes, then add frozen flounder. Cover. Turn off heat. When ready to serve, cook at low boil for 5 minutes. Serves 4.

Lentil Soup — Zuppa di Lenticchie

2 cups lentils
2½ quarts water
¼ cup olive oil
1 cup chopped onions
½ t freshly ground black pepper

¼ cup diced celery
¼ cup chopped parsley
2 t salt
1 bay leaf
1 clove garlic, minced

Wash the lentils and soak in warm water 1 hour. Drain; add the 2½ quarts water. Bring to a boil and cook over low heat 1½ hours.

Heat the oil in a skillet; sauté the onions, garlic, and celery 10 minutes. Add to the soup with parsley, salt, pepper and bay leaf. Cook 10 minutes longer. Taste for seasoning, discard the bay leaf, and serve very hot. *Can use canned lentils to cook quickly.*

Zucchini Soup — Crema di Zucchine

8 small zucchini, diced
1 T butter
1 t olive oil
½ t salt
½ t pepper

1 quart water
4 eggs, lightly beaten
4 T grated Parmesan cheese
1 t chopped parsley
½ t chopped sweet basil

Melt butter in soup pan; add oil, zucchini, salt and pepper and brown lightly. Add water, cover pan and cook 20 minutes. Beat eggs lightly in mixing bowl, add cheese, parsley and basil and blend together well. Remove soup from fire, add egg mixture, stirring it in well, and let stand 3 minutes before serving. Serves 4.

Cucumber Soup — Crema di Cetrioli

4 cucumbers, peeled, seeded, cubed   4 onions, diced

Cover cucumbers and onions with canned chicken broth and 1T generous splash of chicken bullion granules (or 2 cubes). Boil 20 minutes until soft. Cool. Blend mixture. Put in refrigerator until serving time. Serve with a generous spoon of sour cream or yogurt on top. Float a cucumber slice for garnish.

Vegetable and Bread Soup — Ribollita

2 potatoes
2 cups cabbage, shredded
2 cups black cabbage (kale)
4 ripe tomatoes
4 cups fresh cannellini
 beans, canned
1 cup swiss chard
1 red onion
3 cloves garlic

2 sticks celery
2 carrots
2 small zucchini
Rosemary, some sage leaves
4 T extra-virgin olive oil
Bread, a day or two old
Ground black pepper
Salt

Grease a baking sheet. Put the bread on the sheet and bake at 350°F until golden brown, about 15 minutes. Remove from the oven. Cut 1 garlic clove in half and rub on each side of the toast slices. Sprinkle with black pepper and set aside.

It is best to cook the beans on their own first, perhaps the day before, as they cook much more slowly than the rest of the vegetables. Or use canned white beans. Clean, wash, peel and chop all the vegetables and put into a large saucepan. You can add any vegetables you like. Cover with water and cook for 40 minutes. Remove from the heat and add the cooked beans. Fry the onion with the oil and black pepper in a separate pan, add the rosemary and sage leaves. In a casserole, arrange the prepared bread slices on the bottom, cover them with the fried onion and seasonings, and then pour in the soup and cook gently for about ten minutes, then leave to stand off the heat.

Before serving, it should be put in the oven to cook for twenty minutes, with olive oil drizzled on top. You can also garnish the soup with rings of raw onions before putting it into the oven as, once baked, they give a really special flavor to this favorite classic.

Onions

The onion is round. So is a basketball, a grapefruit, a globe, the moon.
How does the onion's roundness differ from theirs?
                    —Nancy Willard

The onion wears a papery sheath.
It is the moon gone to ground,
light enclosed in a brown paper bag,
not really round, but the shape
of the tears we weep when we take
a knife to its white skin.

"Onions," says the *Joy*
of Cooking, "are of easy culture.
They prefer moist, rich earth,
sun, and shallow planting."
It does not say they are the moon's
long-lost relatives who send up
green spears toward the sun.

The grapefruit, on the other hand,
is a little sun. We cut it in half
and pour on sun-colored honey.
The mixture of sweet and tart
waking our tongues, we rise
from the table feeling lighter.

"Onions are supposed to be the secret
of health," says the *Joy of Cooking.*
"But how can they keep that secret?"

Cipolle

La cipolla è tonda. Lo stesso un palla da basket, un pompelmo, un globo, la luna.
Come si differenzia la rotondità della cipolla dalla loro?
—Nancy Willard

La cipolla porta un involucro cartaceo.
È la luna arrivata sulla terra,
luce rinchiusa in una busta di carta marrone,
non proprio tonda, ma della forma
di lacrime che piangiamo quando portiamo
un coltello vicino alla sua pelle bianca.

"Cipolle," dice il libro *Joy*
of Cooking, "sono di facile coltura.
Prediligono l'umido, terreno ricco,
sole, e vanno piantate poco profonde."
Non dice che sono parenti della luna
perduti da tempo, che mandano
verdi lance verso il sole.

Il pompelmo, dall'altra parte,
è un piccolo sole. Lo tagliamo a metà
e ci versiamo del miele dorato.
L'insieme di dolce e aspro
sveglia il palato e ci alziamo
dalla tavola sentendoci leggeri.

"Si pensa che le cipolle siano il segreto
della salute," dice il libro *Joy of Cooking.*
"Ma come possono tenere questo segreto?"

In a cool, dark place they sleep
in their papery shells. Giant pearls,
they will be married to mushrooms.
Fire is the priest at this wedding.

Onions, sliced into rings,
do not bounce, do not sail
through the air and into a hoop
looped round with netting as the crowd
cheers and the sun is captured
for another year.

Onions live more quietly
though they may sizzle
in their bath of oil.

The onion is not painted blue
where oceans pulse
or green where continents sprawl.
The globes of my childhood
are all wrong now--the names
of countries changed, borders
redrawn, but where the soil
is moist and rich, onions
still flourish, tiny illumined
globes in the spinning dark.

— *Nan Fry*

Dormono in un posto fresco e buio,
nel loro guscio di carta. Perle giganti,
si sposeranno coi funghi.
Il fuoco fa da prete a questo connubio.

Le cipolle tagliate ad anelli
non rimbalzano, non navigano
nell'aria e dentro un cerchio
avvolte di rete mentre la folla
acclama ed il sole è catturato
per un altro anno.

Le cipolle vivono più tranquille
nonostante potrebbero sfrigolare
nel loro bagno di olio.

La cipolla non è dipinta di blu
dove pulsano oceani
o di verde dove continenti si distendono.
I globi della mia infanzia
adesso sono tutti sbagliati—i nomi
dei paesi cambiati, confini
ritracciati, ma dove il suolo
è umido e ricco, prosperano
ancora cipolle, piccoli globi
illuminati nel buio che si estende.

— *Nan Fry*
trans: *Sabine Pascarelli*

Love at the Grocery

The worst advice I ever got was
if you're looking for love,
try the produce section at your local grocery.
I've been a vegetarian for two years
and I've never taken a romantic stroll
down the lettuce aisle.
I'm alone from romaine to rapini.
Week after week I dream of my prince.
He'll be wearing faded jeans and a button-down shirt,
preferably periwinkle and he'll have on sandals,
either Tevas or Birks, I can't decide.
He'll be holding a bouquet of broccoli
and a shy smile will tip-toe across his face
as he approaches me. *"It's my favorite,"* he'll say.
"Mine too."
Then he'll slip his arm around me
and we'll fill our buggy with corn and tomatoes,
eggplant and bok choy. Anything that grows
out of earth's belly will be fair game.
We'll measure the days in corn stalks and potato peels
and I'll wear dresses the color of habenero and summer squash.
At our wedding I'll carry a nosegay of cilantro and basil.
We'll push that shopping cart around the aisles,
pointing out produce as if we were on a gondola in Venice.
The sign on the back will read, *Just Cookin'*.

— *Carly Sachs*

Amore nel Supermercato

Il peggior consiglio che ho mai ricevuto era
se sei in cerca di amore
prova al reparto Frutta e Verdura del tuo supermercato.
Sono stata vegetariana per due anni
e mai ho fatto una passeggiatina romantica
lungo il corridoio dell'insalata.
Sono sola dalla romana alle rape.
Settimana dopo settimana sogno il mio principe.
Indosserà jeans sbiancati ed una camicia con bottoncini sul colletto,
preferibilmente blu-*periwinkle*, e porterà sandali,
o *Tevas* oppure *Birkenstock*, non so decidere.
In mano avrà un bouquet di broccoli
e un sorriso timido attraverserà il suo viso in punta di piedi
mentre si avvicinerà a me. "*È il mio preferito,*" dirà.
"*Anche il mio.*"
Poi mi metterà il braccio intorno
e riempiremo il nostro carrello di mais e pomodori,
melanzane e bok choy. Qualsiasi cosa crescerà
dalla pancia della terra sarà di facile bersaglio.
Conteremo i giorni con steli di mais e bucce di patate
ed indosserò abiti color habenero e zucca estiva.
Al nostro matrimonio porterò un bouquet di coriandolo e basilico.
Spingeremo quel carrello della spesa lungo i corridoi,
indicando con la mano i prodotti come se fossimo in una gondola a Venezia.
Il cartello dietro porterà la scritta '*Oggi Cucinati*'.

— *Carly Sachs*
trans: *Sabine Pascarelli*

Saturday Night

There's bread
baking in a blazing

oven. the yeast, active
and alive, perfumes

the kitchen and then
the whole house: the musk

of a woman excited
by her lover's

heat. Flour powders
the blemished

counters as if
an early winter

storm passed through
this room. Wonderful

to experience snow
in a warm climate while

waiting for the loaf
to rise.

— *Karren LaLonde Alenier*

Sabato Sera

C'è pane
che sta cuocendo nel forno

caldissimo. Il lievito, attivo
e vivo, profuma

la cucina e poi
l'intera casa: il muschio

di una donna, eccitata
dal fuoco del suo

amante. Farina cade
sui piani

maculati come
una precoce tempesta

invernale che si abbatte
su questa stanza. Magnifico

sperimentare la neve
in un clima caldo

aspettando che il pane
cresca.

— *Karren LaLonde Alenier*
trans: *Sabine Pascarelli*

FIRST COURSE — PRIMI PIATTI

Gnocchi with Mushrooms and Spinach —
Gnocchi con Funghi e Spinaci

Penne and Cauliflower — Penne al Cavolfiore

Sautéed Porcini Mushrooms with Polenta —
Porcini in Umido con Polenta

Manicotti Venetian Style — Manicotti alla Veneziana

Tagliatelle with Peas and Gorgonzola —
Tagliatelle con Piselli e Gorgonzola

Spaghetti with Bacon — Spaghetti alla Carbonara

Baked Macaroni — Pasta al Forno

Risotto with Safron — Risotto allo Zafferano

Spaghetti with Tuna Fish Sauce — Spaghetti al Tonno

Rice and Beans — Riso e Fagioli

Gnocchi with Mushrooms and Spinach — Gnocchi con Funghi e Spinaci

Gnocchi can be bought at any Italian store or good supermarket.
1 package serves 4 for a 1ˢᵗ course.

1 large onion	½ lb fresh mushrooms, sliced
Minced garlic	3 T olive oil
3 T butter	½ bag baby spinach

Sauté onion and garlic, remove, sauté mushrooms (add oil if needed). Remove. Sauté spinach until limp and almost crisp. Combine all ingredients, keep warm. Gnocchi cooks in 3 minutes, when it rises to top of boiling water. Drain. Toss with toppings. (Add crumbled, cooked bacon for the non-vegetarians). Serve with imported grated cheese (parmesan).

A variation
After boiling gnocchi (3 min.), drain, roll in seasoned bread crumbs, and sauté lightly in butter on all sides. Remove and use sauce of your choice. Also can be put on forks with an Italian sauce for hors d'oeuvres

Penne and Cauliflower — Penne al Cavolfiore

1 medium sized cauliflower
  (or Broccoli or Rape)
Breadcrumbs of fresh bread
1 cup extra-virgin olive oil
2 T freshly chopped parsley

Salt
3 garlic cloves, chopped
1 lb penne
1 dried hot pepper, finely
  chopped

Bring a big enough cooking pot with salted water to a boil. Divide the cauliflower into small flowers and rinse them. When the water boils, drop them in and wait until it boils again, then add the penne. Penne and cauliflower will be cooked at the same moment, drain them in a colander and arrange them in a bowl to be served.

Heat olive oil in a frying pan over medium heat, add the chopped garlic and the chili pepper. A minute before the garlic becomes golden, add the bread crumbs. When they are crisp, pour everything over the cauliflower-pasta. Be careful that the garlic does not get brown. Mix well, then top it with the finely chopped fresh parsley.

(In the same way you can cook other vegetables with penne like broccoli or rape. Important: drop the vegetables in the boiling water, wait until it boils again, then add the penne.) Serves 4-8.

Sautéed Porcini Mushrooms with Polenta – Porcini in Umido con Polenta

The Porcini Mushrooms

1 cup extra-virgin olive oil

1 lb fresh porcini, scrubbed
  with mushroom brush and sliced

Salt and freshly ground black pepper

2 cloves garlic, whole

1 t fresh nepeta leaves
  (or wild mint)

½ cup canned tomatoes, squeezed and with liquid reserved

The Polenta

2 quarts cold water

1 T salt

2 T extra-virgin olive oil

1 lb polenta, coarse ground

Place the water in a large, heavy soup pot and bring to a boil over medium heat. Add the oil and salt.

Stir in the polenta, whisking continuously to prevent lumps and cook for 40 minutes over low heat. Stir frequently using a wooden spoon.

Meanwhile, prepare the mushrooms:

Place the oil in a non-stick skillet. Add the garlic and sauté for 1 minute, stir in the mushrooms, nepeta and cook for 5 minutes over low heat.

Add the tomatoes along with 2 tablespoons of the reserved liquid, salt and pepper and continue to cook for 10 minutes, stirring frequently.

When the polenta comes away from the sides of the pot, remove from heat and distribute among individual bowls. Top with mushrooms and serve.

Manicotti Venetian Style — Manicotti alla Veneziana

1 (8oz) package manicotti noodles
Boiling salted water

1 T cooking oil

Meat filling

1 lb meat-loaf mixture
   (ground pork, beef and veal)
1 large onion, peeled, diced
1 clove garlic, peeled, minced
1 egg, well beaten

1 cup fresh bread crumbs
¼ cup finely chopped parsley
1 t crumbled sweet basil
Salt and pepper

Sauce

6 T butter
6 T flour
½ t salt
White pepper
¼ t ground nutmeg
1½ cup chicken broth

1 cup light cream
¼ cup freshly grated
Parmesan cheese
Nutmeg (to sprinkle)
Chopped parsley

Cook manicotti shells in large pan boiling salted water, with oil floating on surface, 15 minutes, until al dente. Drain well; rinse with cold water. Set aside.

For filling, in heavy skillet cook meat-loaf mixture, onion, and garlic over low heat until meat loses all red color. Break meat into small chunks as it cooks. Drain well. Combine meat mixture, egg, bread crumbs, parsley and seasonings, mix well. Stuff manicotti shells with filling. Place in lightly greased baking dish.

Make sauce in large saucepan. Melt butter; add flour; cook, stirring constantly, until bubbly. Add seasonings; stir well. Add broth and cream all at one time. Cook, stirring constantly, until thickened. Remove from heat; stir in cheese.

Pour sauce evenly over stuffed manicotti noodles. Sprinkle lightly with nutmeg and chopped parsley. Bake at 350°F for 30 minutes. Serve immediately. Makes 6 to 8 servings.

Tagliatelle with Peas and Gorgonzola — Tagliatelle con Piselli e Gorgonzola

1 lb tagliatelle
⅓ cup of gorgonzola (sweet)
1 onion
½ cup of cream

½ cup frozen peas
½ cup of bacon, chopped
1 t butter
Salt, white pepper

In a skillet, fry the bacon in butter, then add the chopped onion, until the bacon gets golden and the onion translucent. Add the peas, stir delicately.

Mix the gorgonzola with the cream until well blended, then pour it into the skillet. Season with salt and pepper. Boil the tagliatelle in salted water, drain in a colander and mix delicately together with the sauce in the skillet. Serves 4-6.

Spaghetti with Bacon — Spaghetti alla Carbonara

4 oz Pancetta, chopped
  (ham or bacon)
3 garlic cloves,
  finely chopped
¼ cup milk (or cream)
6 eggs

⅔ cup Parmesan cheese, grated
Salt and pepper
3 T fresh parsley,
  finely chopped
1 lb spaghetti

Fry the pancetta and garlic in a little olive oil in a very large frying pan (that will also fit the spaghetti) over medium heat until golden. Remove from the heat and put aside. Meanwhile, cook the spaghetti al dente. Whisk together the eggs, parsley and cheese, add the milk. Season with salt and abundant black pepper. Pour the drained spaghetti into the pan with the bacon, over medium heat, then pour in the egg mixture and mix thoroughly. Cook for 2 minutes until the egg mixture thickens a little, but not too much. Serve hot. Serves 4-6.

Baked Macaroni — Pasta al Forno

Sauce

½ lb ground beef	2-3 garlic cloves
1 leek stalk	2 T olive oil
1 onion	1 carrot
2 lbs peeled Italian tomatoes (can)	

With these ingredients, cook a simple Italian meat sauce:

Fry the chopped onion, the garlic, the chopped carrot and the leek in good quality olive oil for a few minutes. Add the ground meat, fry 5 minutes more. Add the peeled tomatoes, crush them with a fork. Season with salt and pepper. Cook the sauce for one hour.

Pasta

1 lb penne	Grated parmesan cheese
2-3 mozzarella balls	

Boil the pasta and drain in a colander. Preheat oven to 350°. Using a baking tray with borders, grease the base to prevent pasta from sticking. Begin layering the pasta on the bottom, cover with a layer of sauce, top with finely cut mozzarella. Cover the last layer with grated parmesan. Place into the preheated oven and cook for about half an hour, or until there will be a light brown crust on the surface. Serves 6.

Risotto with Saffron — Risotto allo Zafferano

½ small onion, finely minced   1 T butter
Pinch of saffron   1 T butter
½ cup long-grain white rice   1 T olive oil
2 T dry white wine   2 cups hot beef broth
2 T grated parmesan cheese

Sauté the onions and rice in the butter and olive oil over moderate heat until very lightly browned. Add the wine and cook until it is absorbed. Dissolve the saffron in the hot beef broth.

Add the beef broth a little at a time and continue to cook, stirring constantly, until all of the liquid is absorbed and the rice is tender and creamy in consistency. This process should take 18 to 20 minutes. Stir in the remaining butter and the parmesan cheese and allow the cheese to melt. Serve immediately. Risotto does not reheat well. Makes 4 servings.

Spaghetti with Tuna Fish Sauce — Spaghetti al Tonno

¼ cup olive oil
½ cup chopped onions
1 clove garlic, minced
1 cup chopped celery
3 - 8 oz cans tomato sauce
1 ¼ t salt
¼ t freshly ground black pepper
¼ t crushed dried red peppers

1 t basil
2 - 7 ¾ oz cans tuna fish,
  drained & broken into chunks
¼ cup capers
½ cup sliced Italian olives
1 lb spaghetti,
  cooked and drained

Heat the oil in a saucepan; sauté the onions 10 minutes. Mix in the garlic, celery, tomato sauce, salt, black pepper, red peppers, and basil. Bring to a boil and cook over low heat 30 minutes. Add the tuna fish, capers, anchovies, and olives. Cook 5 minutes longer. Pour over the hot spa - ghetti. Serves 4-6.

Easy Version

1 large can tuna
1 pint canned tomatoes
  + 1 cup spaghetti sauce
4T parsley

Olive oil
Garlic powder
1 large onion
Salt and pepper

Dice onion, sauté in olive oil and butter. When translucent, add tuna with its juice, sprinkle with garlic powder, salt and pepper, and sauce liberally. Add fresh parsley (No other herbs!)

Simmer 15 minutes — if more fluid needed, add splash tomato juice, V-8, or chicken bouillon in water.

Rice and Beans — Riso con Fagioli

¼ cup olive oil
1 carrot
1 stalk celery
½ cup chopped parsley
½ t freshly ground black pepper
1 twig of fresh rosemary
  in ½ cup of olive oil
1 - 1 lb can kidney beans
2 cups boiling water

¾ cup chopped onions
1 leek
1 clove garlic, minced
2 - 8 oz cans tomato sauce, or
  2 lb can tomatoes, peeled
½ t freshly ground black
  pepper
1 cup rice
Grated Romano or
  Parmesan cheese

Heat the oil in a saucepan; sauté the onions, carrot, celery and leek for 5 minutes. Add the garlic and parsley; sauté 5 minutes longer. Mix in the tomato sauce, 1½ cups water, the salt and pepper; cook over low heat 30 minutes. Add the beans; cook 10 minutes.

While the sauce is cooking, cook the rice in the boiling water 15 minutes. Drain well. Mix into the sauce and beans; cook 5 minutes longer. Add rosemary oil with twig removed. Taste for seasoning. Serve with the cheese. Serves 6-8.

Linguini

It was always linguini between us.
Linguini with white sauce, or
red sauce, sauce with basil snatched from
the garden, oregano rubbed between
our palms, a single bay leaf adrift amidst
plum tomatoes. Linguini with meatballs,
sausage, a side of brascioli. Like lovers
trying positions, we enjoyed it every way
we could-artichokes, mushrooms, little
neck clams, mussels, and calamari-linguini
twining and braiding us each to each.
Linguini knew of the kisses, the smooches,
the *molti baci*. It was never spaghetti
between us, not cappellini, nor farfalle,
vermicelli, pappardelle, fettucini, perciatelli,
or even tagliarini. Linguini we stabbed, pitched,
and twirled on forks, spun round and round
on silver spoons. Long, smooth, and always
al dente. In dark trattorias, we broke crusty panera,
toasted each other — *La dolce vita!* — and sipped
Amarone, wrapped ourselves in linguini,
briskly boiled, lightly oiled, salted, and lavished
with sauce. *Bellissimo, paradisio, belle gente!*
Linguini witnessed our slurping, pulling, and
sucking, our unraveling and raveling, chins
glistening, napkins tucked like bibs in collars,
linguini stuck to lips, hips, and bellies, cheeks
flecked with *formaggio* — parmesan, romano,
and shaved pecorino — strands of linguini flung
around our necks like two fine silk scarves.

— *Diane Lockward*

Linguine

C'erano sempre le linguine tra di noi.
Linguine con salsa bianca o
salsa rossa, salsa con basilico strappato
dall'orto, origano strofinato tra
le nostre mani, una sola foglia d'alloro alla deriva
in mezzo ai pomodorini. Linguine con polpettine,
salsiccia, tagliata di braciola. Come amanti
che provano posizioni, ce le gustavamo in ogni
possibile maniera — con carciofi, funghi,
arselle, cozze, e calamari — linguine
ci avvolgevano e ci legavano l'uno all'altra.
Linguine sapevano di baci, di sbaciucchiamenti,
di *molti baci.* Non c'erano mai spaghetti
tra di noi, né cappellini, né farfalle,
vermicelli, pappardelle, fettuccine, perciatelli,
e nemmeno tagliolini. Linguine trafitte, inforcate
e arrotolate su forchette, girate e rigirate
su cucchiai d'argento. Lunghe, lisce e sempre
al dente. In buie trattorie abbiamo spezzato pane
croccante, brindato — *La dolce vita!* — e sorseggiato
Amarone, avvolgendoci nelle linguine, cotte su
fiamma vivace, con poco olio, sale, ed abbondante
sugo. *Bellissimo, paradiso, bella gente!*
Linguine, testimoni del nostro sorbire, tirar su e
succhiare, del nostro sbrogliare e aggrovigliare, menti
lucidi, tovaglioli legati al collo come bavaglini,
linguine che aderivano a labbra, fianchi e addomi, le
guance macchiate di *formaggio* — parmigiano,
romano e trucioli di pecorino — fili di linguine avvolti
intorno al collo come due delicati foulard di seta.

— *Diane Lockward*
trans: *Sabine Pascarelli*

Risotto

I make Risotto

in an old brass pot.

My mother,

adding a dash of this and that

to all she cooks

thinks me grand

I am not.

I am making Risotto

in an old brass pot .

— *Michael S. Glaser*

Risotto

Faccio il risotto

in una vecchia pentola d'ottone.

Mia madre, aggiungendo

un pizzico di questo e di quello

a tutto ciò che cucina

mi ritiene grandioso

Non lo sono.

Sto facendo il risotto

in una vecchia pentola d'ottone.

— *Michael S. Glaser*
trans: *Sabine Pascarelli*

Making Lasagna

stalks of lilac stoop to face
perfection in a ruined vase

kettles simmer on the stove
while candles alter air to gold

the drape of semolina's sheets
laid gently over pillowed sheep's

medallions melt in rising heat
and heft of pomodoro, sweet

incessant stirrings sated soon
held in hungers' pleasure swoon

— *Emily Ferrara*

Facendo Lasagne

steli di lillà si chinano per guardare
la perfezione in un vaso rovinato

tegami in lenta cottura sui fornelli
mentre le candele rendono l'aria dorata

lenzuola drappeggiate di semola
dolcemente s'adagiano su cucini di formaggio,

medaglioni, che si sciolgono nel bollore,
affondano nel dolce pomodoro

girando incessantemente, sarà presto
saziata la fame in deliquio di piacere

— *Emily Ferrara*
trans: *Sabine Pascarelli*

Wine

Sometimes wine is a river you flower in,
the tight buds of your lips opening
to sip, to swallow a dark sun in.

You smile as the world unmoors itself
and words float out in unfamiliar
tongues. The grape's too perfect

to resist–its supple globes, its goblet air,
its hard vines snaking from the blood-fed
soil. You could be Bacchus calling in

the saints: full-bodied St. Estephe,
or sprightly St. Emilion. They swirl
and burn, the river rising inside you

till there you are, brim, half-bobbing
with affection, laughter, half-drowning,
kissing, saying, *yes, my darling, yes,*

the dock a long way off, the bow line gone.

— *Christina Daub*

Vino

Talvolta il vino è un fiume nel quale fiorisci,
i compatti boccioli delle tue labbra si aprono
per sorseggiare, per ingoiare un sole scuro.

Tu sorridi mentre il mondo leva gli ormeggi
e parole si librano in insolite
lingue. L'uva è troppo perfetta

per resistere ai suoi arrendevoli globi,
il suo aspetto di calice,
i suoi duri tralci che si snodano dal terreno
concimato con sangue. Potresti essere Bacco

che chiama i Santi: il corposo St. Estephe,
o il brioso St. Emilion. Essi turbinano
e bruciano, il fiume cresce in te

finché non sei colmo, ballonzolando
con garbo, con risate, mezzo annegato,
baciando, dicendo *si, tesoro mio, si,*

il molo ormai lontano, la linea di prua sparita.

— *Christina Daub*
trans: *Sabine Pascarelli*

SECOND COURSE — SECONDI PIATTI

Chicken Marsala — Pollo al Marsala

Chicken Cacciatore — Pollo alla Cacciatora

Beefsteak Rolls — Involtini di Carne

Tuscan Stew — Spezzatino Toscano

Nettie's Cabbage Rolls — Involtini di Verza alla "Nettie"

Fish Baked in Aluminum Foil — Pesce nel Cartoccio

Fish Filets in Tomato Sauce — Filetti di Pesce al Pomodoro

Pork Roast in Chianti — Arrosto di Maiale al Chianti

Cold Veal in Tuna Sauce — Vitello Tonnato

Braised Beef in BAROLO Sauce — Brasato al BAROLO

Chicken Marsala — Pollo al Marsala

1 roasting chicken, disjointed
1 t salt
¼ t freshly ground black pepper
2 T butter
2 T olive oil
½ cup minced onions
½ cup Marsala wine or sweet sherry
½ t freshly ground black pepper

½ cup sliced mushrooms
1 clove garlic, minced
1 bay leaf
½ t thyme
3 sprigs parsley
1 T flour
2 T water
2 T capers

Season the chicken with salt and pepper. Heat the butter and oil in a casserole; add the chicken and onions. Cover and cook over low heat 20 minutes, without browning turn the chicken once. Add the wine, broth, mushrooms, garlic, bay leaf, thyme, and parsley. Cover and cook over low heat 45 minutes or until tender. Transfer chicken to a platter and keep warm. Discard bay leaf and parsley. Mix the flour and water; stir into the sauce until thickened.

Chicken Cacciatore — Pollo alla Cacciatora

8 chicken thighs (boned and skinned)
⅓ cup olive oil
1 large clove garlic — crushed
2 onions, finely sliced
½ cup boiling water
2 bay leaves

4 t tomato paste or a splash of
  spaghetti sauce
⅔ cup white wine, red wine or
  port
Salt and pepper
1 beef bullion cube

Brown garlic in oil. Sauté chicken, remove, keep warm. Add onion, sauté. Add parsley. Add bullion, tomato paste and seasoning. Add wine. Replace chicken — cover. Simmer for 30 minutes — add a little bullion, wine or water if it thickens. Serves 4-6.

Beefsteak Rolls — Involtini di Carne

8 slices fillet of beef, ¾ inch thick
8 thin slices mozzarella cheese
½ cup flour
½ t freshly ground black pepper
1 cup dry bread crumbs
1 cup beef broth
1 T grated parmesan cheese

8 slices prosciutto or boiled
   ham
1 ½ t salt
1 egg, beaten
5 T butter
1 t meat extract
½ T chopped parsley

Cut each slice of beef horizontally through the middle, leaving one end closed. In the opening place 1 slice ham and 1 slice mozzarella cheese. Press the open sides together. Roll in flour mixed with the salt and pepper. (Reserve 1 tablespoon.) Dip into egg, then roll in the bread crumbs. Roll up and fasten with toothpicks. Melt 4 tablespoons butter in a skillet; brown the steaks on both sides.

Melt the remaining butter in a saucepan; blend in the reserved flour thoroughly and add 1 cup beef broth. Cook over low heat 3 minutes; mix in the meat extract. Remove from heat and stir in the parmesan cheese and parsley. Arrange the rolls on serving dish and pour the sauce over them. Serves 8.

Tuscan Stew — Spezzatino Toscano

2 lbs. veal, cut into cubes   1 lb. onions (half the weight of
  (½ lb. each person)   the meat), cut into rings
2 bay leaves   6 cloves
Salt, abundant pepper   1 T butter
4 slices of rusk, well crumbled (hard, sweet biscuit)

Melt the butter in a large cooking pot, add the onion rings and let them
become translucent. Add the meat cubes and the seasonings. Cover with
water. Simmer for about 2 hours. 20 minutes before ready, stir in the
crumbled rusk, to thicken the sauce. Serve with boiled potatoes and
salad. Serves 4.

Nettie's Cabbage Rolls — Involtini di Verza alla "Nettie"

1 head cabbage   basil
1 cup cooked rice   garlic
1 lb. ground meat   grated cheese
1 egg   tomato sauce
1 cup bread crumbs   mixed Italian seasonings
  (ground or bought)

Parboil a head of cabbage, turn often. Takes 30 minutes or more.
    In a bowl mix ground roundsteak, bread crumbs, egg, cooked rice,
Italian seasonings (purchased: combines oregano, sage, thyme, parsley).
Mix in parmesan, grated cheese, salt and pepper. Make a ball of this
mixture. Take one leaf of cabbage and place ball of meat in center. Tuck
cabbage in from both sides, then roll and squeeze juice out tightly. They
should stay together — handle gently. If center of cabbage is hard, put
leaves back for more boiling.
    When all leaves are filled and rolled, lay in large pan for stove top
or in oven at 350°. Cover with tomato sauce and simmer for 1 hour.

Fish Baked in Aluminium Foil — Pesce al Cartoccio

For each person

1 fish (like trout, mullet) cleaned
    from scales, interiors removed
1 potato, peeled and cut into slices
1-2 garlic cloves

Some sage leaves
Small rosemary sprig
Salt, pepper
Extra virgin olive oil

Preheat oven to 375°

Prepare in a large enough piece of aluminum foil, square format, for each portion.

Place in center potato slices, to cover the space the fish will take. Season with salt and pepper and sprinkle with olive oil.

Arrange the fish on the potato slices. Stuff the fish with garlic cloves, sage and rosemary sprig. Season with salt and pepper, sprinkle with oil.

Close the foil very well, then put the wrapped fish portions side by side on a large baking pan.

Bake for approx. 45 minutes. Serve each portion with the foil, lightly unfolded, on a plate.

Fish Filets in Tomato Sauce — Filetti di Pesce al Pomodoro

1 lb. fish filets (frozen are easiest)	Chili powder
3 stalks celery	Saffron
1 can tomatoes	Paprika
1 large onion	Curry
½ cup chicken broth	Ginger
6 broccoli florets	Turmeric
¼ cup olive oil	Garlic powder

Sauté fish in olive oil, (flounder, cod, snapper, sole, trout, whiting). In a separate pan, boil vegetables until soft in 1 can diced tomatoes and broth. Add pinches of saffron, paprika, curry, ginger, turmeric, chili powder and garlic powder. Simmer. Add fish.

Pork Roast in Chianti — Arrosto di Maiale al Chianti

1 - 4 lb boned, rolled and tied pork roast	1 ½ cups Chianti wine
2 T lemon juice	1 clove garlic, minced
1 t dried basil, crumbled	1 t dried rosemary, crumbled
1- 8 oz can tomato sauce	3 T olive oil
	Salt and pepper, to taste

Wipe the pork roast with a damp cloth. Place in a glass or porcelain container or heavy duty freezer bag. Combine the Chianti, garlic, lemon juice, rosemary, and basil and pour over the meat. Cover and marinate in the refrigerator for 24 hours, turning occasionally (if using a plastic bag, close with a twist-tie).

Bring the roast to room temperature before cooking. Remove the roast from the marinade and pat dry. Reserve the marinade. Heat the oil in large heavy Dutch oven. Brown the roast well on all sides.

Combine the marinade and the tomato sauce, salt and pepper and pour over the meat. Cook in 375° oven, 0 minutes per pound.

Cold Veal in Tuna Sauce — Vitello Tonnato

This is one of THE classic summer dishes, and is also the traditional centerpieces of the Ferragosto dinner.

This dish consists of thin slices of roasted or braised veal, served cold with creamy mayonnaise sauce containing tuna, capers and anchovies.

Ingredients for 4 servings:

1 ½ lbs veal rump roast	1 onion
Salt	1 celery stalk
2 carrots	1 stock cube (bullion)

For the tuna sauce:

Large can of tuna in oil	2 T capers
2 anchovy fillets	1 cup mayonnaise

A few more capers, some lemon slices,
    and sprigs of parsley for garnishing

Put the meat into a saucepan just large enough to hold it. Add the carrots, celery, bullion and salt. Add just enough water to cover, and bring slowly to a boil. Simmer the meat for one hour or until fork-tender. When the veal is cooked, remove the pot from the heat and let the meat cool in the stock. When the veal is cold, remove it from the broth, slice thinly and set aside.

For the tuna sauce: Drain the tuna and put into a food processor with anchovies, capers and mayonnaise. Process for 30 seconds at medium speed until it becomes a creamy sauce. If made ahead of time, refrigerate.

Lay the slices out on one or more platters (you want just one layer). Spread the sauce over the meat, garnish the platters with some lemon slices, capers and parsley. Cover them with plastic wrap, and chill them in the refrigerator before serving.

Variation: At the very end, add ½ pound of strawberries (best if small wood-strawberries, but also normal strawberries are fine) to the tuna mixture, process all together. Garnish with some of the strawberries instead of lemon slices.

Braised Beef with BAROLO Sauce — Brasato al BAROLO

2 lbs. beef rump	1 bouquet parsley
1 onion, minced	1 bottle BAROLO wine
2 carrots, minced	2 T tomato concentrate
2 leek stalks, minced	Broth
1 garlic clove, minced	4 T extra-virgin olive oil
2 bay leaves	Salt, pepper

1. Put the meat in a bowl, add the minced onion, carrots, leek, garlic, the seasonings and the wine. Cover and let marinate overnight in a cool place.
2. Heat 4 tbsp of olive oil in a sauce pan, add the beef drained from its liquids and let it brown on all sides. Add the marinate with vegetables and seasonings and let boil over high heat so that the liquid restrains a little.
3. Add the tomato concentrate previously melted in a little broth, add salt, pepper and simmer for about 3 hours, turning the meat from time to time. If necessary, add more broth. When tender, remove the beef from the pan (keep warm), remove bay leaves and rosemary and blend the sauce.
4. Serve the meat cut in slices with half of the sauce on top, serve the remaining sauce in a gravy boat.

Can be accompanied by polenta, mashed potatoes or boiled potatoes.

The Poets In My Life Meet On The Third Sunday

They bring fettuccini or humus
Roast Lamb or water cress salad
Bright with nasturtium flowers

They bring bounty from Farmer's Markets
Miner's lettuce, pineapple guavas or mangos
Or doughnuts from the corner store

They bring pontoons or sonnets
Formal verse or free
On crisp white paper

The poets in my life meet on the third Sunday
They bring laughter and tears
They bring love

— *Jean Emerson*

I Poeti nella mia Vita s'incontrano la Terza Domenica

Loro portano fettuccine o crema di ceci
Agnello arrosto o insalata di crescione
Resa vivace con fiori di nasturzio

Portano bontà dai mercati contadini
Lattuga dei minatori, ananas, guava o mango
Oppure *doughnuts* dal negozio all'angolo

Portano *pontoons* o sonetti
Versi formali o liberi
Su briosa carta bianca

I poeti nella mia vita s'incontrano la terza domenica
Portano riso e lacrime
Portano amore

— *Jean Emerson*
trans: *Sabine Pascarelli*

A Gourmand's Prayer

Yellowtail snapper with citrus beurre blanc, filet
mignon in demi-glace cabernet, roast duck garnished
with mint jellied peaches, angels on horseback — dates
stuffed with garlic cloves wrapped in bacon and served
in a hot honey-pepper sauce, bananas foster, key
lime pie, dense, flourless chocolate cake drizzled
with a raspberry coulis, Lord, grant me the power
to well digest all that I have well eaten.

— *Barbara Goldberg*

Preghiera di un Gourmand

Snapper a pinna gialla con citrus beurre blanc, filet
mignon in demi-glace cabernet, anatra arrosto guarnita
di pesche con gelatina di menta, tartine di ostriche — datteri
ripieni di spicchi d'aglio, avvolti in bacon e serviti
in una salsa di miele e pepe, banana flambé, torta
di key-lime, denso dolce di cioccolato senza farina, asperso
di coulis di lampone, Dio, concedimi la forza
di digerire bene le bontà che ho mangiato.

— *Barbara Goldberg*
trans: *Sabine Pascarelli*

To The Wine-Taster

Dionysus would slap you silly
if he could see you now — sniffing
and twirling and sipping and, dear god,
spitting it out. What mortal arrogance,
the mess you've made of his gift. Now,

let's start over. Throw back your head
and drain this puny glass with one loud gulp.
Then send — no, roar — for a cup carved
out of animal horn, deep enough that
when you reach the bottom, you'll see

two horns, two hands, two mouths. Then
you'll be worthy to grab the woman
on your left — who feels, as you do, now,
the rush of sweet blood to the brain and to
the thighs — and put your grape-stained mouth

to hers. We are, all of us, nothing more
than empty vessels that the god can fill
with his heart-made, heart-poured wine. Drink,
you fool, and love. Become divine.

— *Rose Solari*

All'Assaggiatore di Vini

Dionisio ti farebbe morbido
se ti potesse vedere— annusando,
roteando e sorseggiando e, mio dio,
risputando. Con che mortale arroganza
hai sciupato il suo dono. Dunque,

iniziamo da capo. Metti la testa all'indietro
e vuota questo misero bicchiere d'un solo fiato.
Poi fai portare — con un ruggito — una coppa
ricavata da un corno animale, così profonda che
quando arrivi al fondo, vedrai

due corna, due mani, due bocche. Allora
sarai degno di afferrare la donna
alla tua sinistra — che avverte come te, ora,
l'afflusso del suo dolce sangue al cervello e alle
cosce — e posare la tua bocca macchiata di vino

sulla sua. Noi siamo, tutti noi, nient'altro
che vasi vuoti che il dio può riempire
con il suo vino, fatto e versato col cuore. Bevi,
sciocco, ed ama. Diventa divino.

— *Rose Solari*
trans: *Sabine Pascarelli*

VEGETABLES — VERDURE

Roasted Potatoes alla "Angelo" — Patate Arroste alla "Angelo"

Baked Zucchini — Zucchine al Forno

Grilled Eggplant — Melanzane Grigliate

Wilted Spinach — Spinaci Saltati

Italian Peas — Piselli e Pancetta

Spinach/Potatoes Tin — Teglia di Spinaci e Patate

Italian String Beans I — Fagiolini con Cipolle e Pomodori

Italian String Beans II — Fagiolini in Salsa Rossa

Mixed Fried Vegetables — Fritto Misto di Verdure

Rich Summer Vegetables — Ratatuglia Ricca

Stewed Tomatoes — Pomodori Ripieni

Asparagus alla Farnesina — Asparagi alla Farnesina

Roasted Potatoes alla "Angelo" — Patate Arroste alla "Angelo"

3 large baking potatoes
Salt and pepper
Butter

Garlic powder
Olive oil

Scrub potatoes — remove spots in skin. Cut across in rounds ½ inch thick. Lay on greased foil/pans. Dot each top with butter, salt and pepper. Sprinkle garlic powder on each, drizzle with olive oil over all. Preheat oven to 350°, bake for 1 hour, maybe a few minutes longer until soft and browned — not hard.

Alternative:
Peel potatoes. Cut into thirds, lengthwise. Lay on greased foil, dot top side with above seasonings. Turn every 20 minutes and repeat seasoning on each side, in turn. Preheat oven to 350°. Bake for 1 hour, a little more if not brown.

Baked Zucchini — Zucchine al Forno

3 zucchini
1 T vinegar
2 stirred egg whites

6 T seasoned breadcrumbs
1 T olive oil
1/8 cup grated cheese

Mix ½ t each: Parsley, basil, sage, oregano (or buy Italian seasoning)

Wash and cut zucchini and trim ends. Cut each in half lengthwise. Dip in egg and then breadcrumbs. Lay on greased aluminum foil, skin down. Sprinkle herbs and grated cheese — drizzle oil and vinegar on top (may add crushed croutons). Bake at 400° for 15 minutes, then 325° for 30 minutes. Serves 6.

Grilled Eggplant — Melanzane Grigliate

1 large eggplant — peel. Cut lengthwise into sixths. Marinate by sprinkling liberally with vinegar, soy sauce, olive oil, add ground sage, rosemary, parsley, oregano, basil, thyme, tarragon, grated cheese. Turn in liquid all day — eggplant absorbs so you may have to supplement.

When ready to cook, put on grill and turn until done — 30 minutes — or in broiler 10 minutes each side. Serves 4.

Wilted Spinach — Spinaci Saltati

Large bag washed spinach
Salt and pepper

1 ¼ cup olive oil in 2 pans
1 T garlic powder

Warm oil — lay dry spinach in each pan. Season each. Put heat up high, and then turn off. Serve under fish or in omelets. Serves 4.

Italian Peas — Piselli e Pancetta

2 boxes frozen peas	3 strips bacon
2 cloves garlic	1 large onion
¼ cup olive oil	1/8 cup butter
1 T parsley	Salt and pepper

Blanche and drain peas well. Chop and fry onion and bacon together in oil with garlic until crisp. Add peas. Add parsley and seasonings, salt, pepper and butter. Cover. Cook slowly 30 minutes. Serves 6.

Alternate Version:
Use butter substitute and cook bacon separately to crumble in at end.

Spinach/Potatoes Tin — Teglia di Spinaci e Patate

2 lbs frozen spinach	Instant mashed potatoes, for 6
8 slices bacon, fried and crumbled	Tasty cheese that melts
Grated parmesan	(smoked cheese)

Boil spinach in salted water and prepare the mashed potatoes.

Butter a heat-resistant glassware, put half of the mashed potatoes in a thin layer.

Mix the boiled and well-drained spinach with the crumbled bacon and the chopped cheese, then layer it upon the mashed potatoes and cover with another potato layer. Sprinkle with abundant grated parmesan. Bake in preheated oven at 350° until the surface is golden (20–25 minutes.) Serves 6.

Italian String Beans I — Fagiolini con Cipolle e Pomodori

3-4 T olive oil
1 large onion, cut in rings
2 cloves garlic

1 lb. fresh string beans
3 fresh tomatoes, chopped
Salt, pepper

Wash and trim beans, boil in salted water for 30 minutes. Fry onion rings in olive oil until crisp. Remove and keep aside. In the same oil, fry the garlic cloves, add the chopped tomatoes. Fry for 2-3 minutes.

Arrange the string beans in a bowl, drizzle with olive oil. Top with tomatoes, then at last with the onion rings. Can be served hot or cold. Mix quickly just in the moment of serving. Serves 6.

Italian String Beans II — Fagiolini in Salsa Rossa

1 lb. fresh string beans
1 quart water (cover beans)
2 cups spaghetti sauce

1 T each parsley, basil, thyme,
    oregano
bullion

Wash and trim beans — cover with liquids. Add 4 beef bullion cubes. Add spices. Cook slowly until all liquid has gone. Serves 6 to 8.

Mixed Fried Vegetables — Fritto Misto di Verdure

Cauliflower	Potatoes
Artichoke hearts	Zucchini

Prepare the vegetables, chop them into medium size pieces or slices.

Prepare batter with:

2 ¼ cup all-purpose flour	2 fresh eggs
2 oz. beer	Salt

Drop the pieces of vegetables into the batter, then fry until crisp and golden. A good side dish for fried or grilled meats.

Rich Summer Vegetables — Ratatuglia Ricca

1 ½ lb red, yellow and green peppers, chopped	1 lb fresh tomatoes, chopped
2 medium sized eggplants, chopped	4 medium sized zucchini, chopped
2 onions, chopped	2 garlic cloves
Black olives, cut 2–3	6 t olive oil
Salt	Ground pepper

Heat the olive oil in a large frying pan that will hold all vegetables. Fry garlic cloves, add onions until translucent. Add all the other chopped vegetables and the olives, and let simmer on low heat for 45 minutes. Stir. Add salt and pepper at the end. Serves 6.

Stewed Tomatoes — Pomodori Ripieni

8 fresh tomatoes
1/8 lb butter
Salt and pepper
1 T olive oil

½ cup of mixed herbs (parsley,
basil and garlic ground
together)

Cut tomatoes across in half. Scoop out seeds. Lay first layer in large pan. In place of seeds add the herb mixture and a dot of butter in each pocket. Place another layer of tomatoes on top. Drizzle with olive oil. Put ¼ cup water in bottom of pan, cover and cook on low for 45 minutes. Serves 4-6.

Asparagus alla Farnesina — Asparagi alla Farnesina

2 lbs. green asparagus
10 slices of cheddar or similar cheese

10 slices of cooked ham
2–3 T butter

Bechamel sauce, prepared with:
4T butter
Salt and pepper

4T all purpose flour
2 cups milk, nutmeg

Remove the hard end of the asparagus. Bind them together and boil in a small, high cooking pot, heads up, in salted water for 15 minutes. Drain and let them cool.

Take 2 to 3 asparagus at a time and roll them into a slice of cheese, then into a slice of ham, and fix with toothpick.

Arrange the asparagus rolls one beside the other in a greased glassware dish. Cover with the béchamel sauce. Top with butter flakes, sprinkle with ground pepper and nutmeg.

Cook for 20 minutes in a 350° preheated oven, until surface nicely colored. Serve hot. Serves 6.

Green Beans

"The bean is a graceful, confiding, engaging vine;   but you
   never can put beans into poetry. . . .there is no dignity in the bean."
                                    — Charles Dudley Warner

(1)

Spring-loaded vines
on tendrils
shinny up skinny
poles and
shoot for the sun.
Their leavings are
heart shapes that
pinch to life
small yellow crescents
that plump
like the knuckles
on babies' hands.
Each nub
lengthens down
to a green
velvet composure
that will curtsy
and sway in the wind.

(2)

No need to slit the tight skin
down to its pearls. Just snap

the stem and bite. The coldest
spring water never rinses away

Fagiolini Verdi

"Il fagiolino è un grazioso, confidente, simpatico rampicante;   mai però puoi mettere i fagiolini nella poesia. . . .non c'è alcuna dignità nel fagiolo."
— Charles Dudley Warner

(1)
Rampicanti con carica a molla
sui viticci
s'inerpicano su
scarni pali
con rapidità verso il sole.
I loro getti sono
a forma di cuore che
spingono alla nascita
piccole mezzelune gialle
che si gonfiano
come le nocche
sulle mani di neonati.
Ogni sporgenza
si allunga in basso
ad una verde
e vellutata compostezza
che s'inchinerà
ed oscillerà nel vento.

(2)
Non bisogna recidere la stretta buccia
fino alle sue perle. Basta staccare

il gambo e mordere. La più fredda
acqua di fonte non potrà mai lavar via

the holy scent of turned earth
slendered into a bean, that trace

it holds of wild green smoke.
Relaxed in steam and slathered

in buttery gold, each one of
these peasants, when summoned

to the royal red silk
banquet hall of your mouth

will loyally serve its fare,
presenting with quiet dignity

small mists of sweetgrass, pineroot,
peat, seawater, ancient stone.

— *Rod Jellema*

l'odore sacro di terra zappata
assottigliato in un fagiolo, che conserva

tracce di selvatico fumo verde.
Rilassato nel vapore e annegato

in burroso oro, ognuna di
queste contadine, quando convocata

alla maestosa rosso-seta
sala dei banchetti della tua bocca,

adempierà lealmente ai suoi doveri,
presentando con calma dignità

lievi nebbioline di erba agrodolce, radice di pino,
torba, acqua di mare, antica pietra.

— *Rod Jellema*
trans: *Sabine Pascarelli*

From My Sister's Garden

Hot dirt in August burns barefeet,
cukes prick our fingers as we pick.

The lush tomatoes are all but gone
before we spy it — one juicy Beefsteak

peaking through those fuzzy curling leaves
where aphids urge the plant's surrender.

Red, squat, and plump, it waits until
I lift it up. Kitchen-bound, I rinse it cold,

bright water beading on its skin, and
then I choose the sharpest knife to

slice it through with ease. And so,
Tomato, do what you're made for:

bleed your succulence now into my hand.

— *Patricia Gray*

Dal Giardino di mia Sorella

La terra calda brucia i piedi nudi
i cetrioli pungono le dita mentre li cogliamo.

I rigogliosi pomodori sono quasi tutti finiti
poi lo scorgiamo — un succoso *Cuor di Bue*

spunta attraverso arricciate foglie pelose
piene di afidi che spingono la pianta ad arrendersi.

Rosso, tozzo e carnoso aspetta che
lo sollevo. Ritornando in cucina, lo lavo,

acqua chiara gli imperla la buccia, per poi
scegliere il coltello più affilato che

possa affettarlo con facilità. E quindi,
Pomodoro, fa quello per cui sei nato:

sanguina adesso la tua sugosità nella mano mia.

— *Patricia Gray*
trans: *Sabine Pascarelli*

Cynara scolymus

To
learn
to eat
artichokes
is almost as tough
as figuring out how to cook
these space-alien thistle-things, protected outside
by leaves stabby as dragon scales,
and inside too by
bristles you
don't want
to eat.

Gourmet
suggests
clipping off
all the outer leaves
(the purplish ones, thick and sharp)
and peeling the stem as if it were a potato.
Thus denuded, they're ready for
the enterprising
chef to braise,
roast, or
fry them.

No. He
plunges
them intact
in boiling water
that dazzles to emerald as

Cynara scolymus

Im-
parare a
mangiare
il carciofo è
tanto duro quanto
cercare di capire come cucinare
questi extraterrestri simili al cardo, protetti all'esterno
da foglie pungenti come scaglie di drago,
e anche all'interno, da
una peluria che
non vorresti
mangiare.

Gourmet
suggerisce
di eliminare le
foglie più esterne
(quelle purpuree, spesse e acuminate)
e di sbucciare il gambo come se fosse una patata.
Così denudati sono pronti perché
l'intraprendente chef
li possa brasare,
arrostire o
friggere.

No.
Li butta
integri
in acqua bollente
che risplende di verde smeraldo quando

they give up their essence. When they've cooled, he plucks a leaf,
scrapes the tender flesh with his teeth.
Layer by layer we strip
them bare right
down to
the
heart.

— *Moira Egan*

liberano la loro essenza. Una volta raffreddati, egli stacca
una foglia, raschia la tenera polpa con i denti.
Strato dopo strato, li
spogliamo dalle
foglie fino ad
arrivare al
cuore.

— *Moira Egan*
trans: *Sabine Pascarelli*

Choices

*"The day after my grandfather died,
my grandmother ate mushrooms for the first time in 60 years."*
Overheard remark.

Did she forage
in the understory on pearly
summer mornings, the bright
orange crenellations spelling chanterelles,
each year's growth springing up
untouched, for the man who refused
to taste, smell, touch
a mushroom.

Did she dream
of morels, tiny colonies of fragrant
cells, bubbling in butter,
while her body lay cupped inside his
in that long marriage of sleep. Did she
awaken in the hollow of the night
following the liminal smell of porcini
floating in broth, only to slowly sense
his sleeping body, the sweet
scent of him in the dark.

Would she, perhaps,
while he was far in the fields
turn to the unstained pages
of cookbooks — the pristine sections

Scelte

"Il giorno dopo che morì mio nonno,
mia nonna mangiò funghi per la prima volta in 60 anni."
Commento colto per caso.

      Avrà frugato
in precedenti esperienze nelle perlacee
mattinate estive, le vivide
merlature arancioni, dette finferli,
la crescita di ogni anno venendo su
inviolata, per l'uomo che rifiutò
di assaggiare, sentire, toccare
un fungo.

      Avrà sognato
le morchelle, piccole colonie di cellule
profumate, spumeggiando in burro,
mentre il suo corpo giacque rannicchiato in quello di lui
in quel lungo matrimonio di sonno. Si sarà
svegliata nel profondo della notte
seguendo il liminale odore dei porcini
galleggiando in brodo, solo per accorgersi lentamente
del suo corpo dormente, il dolce
profumo di lui nell'oscurità.

      Si sarà forse dedicata,
mentre lui era lontano nei campi,
a sfogliare le immacolate pagine
dei libri di cucina — rubriche intatte

lying flat between the rippled recipes
for seasons of puddings and roasts.

On the morning
after the first night she'd slept alone
in sixty years, did she rise early,
pull her boots over stiff ankles,
take herself to the harsh chill
of the store to finger musty piles
of creminis, umbrellas of portobellos,
little moons of common mushrooms,
the memory of earth on her hands.
And did she return to the cold house —
to the song of butter in the pan,
to mushrooms on toast.

— *Katherine Williams*

distese tra le ricette ondulate
di stagioni di budini ed arrosti.

       La mattina
dopo la prima notte che dormì sola
in sessant'anni, si sarà alzata presto,
tirando gli stivali su caviglie irrigidite,
dirigendosi verso l'inclemente freddo
del negozio per tastare ammuffiti cumuli
di *cremini,* ombrelli di *portobello,*
piccole lune di funghi comuni,
memoria di terra nelle sue mani.
E sarà poi tornata alla fredda casa —
al canto del burro nella padella,
a funghi su pane abbrustolito.

— *Katherine Williams*
trans: *Sabine Pascarelli*

Ode on a Beet

> *All ye need to know*
> — John Keats

Boil raw beets for the pleasure
of it, the old way of it, the work of it,
curly green leaves whistling
to bloody veins. Sunflowers race
for sky, untrellised peas languish,
but beets survive shade of cucumber
too nearly planted. Into yoga, beets

don't fight for space, or compete
with zucchini. Beet nubs heave,
grow, big or tiny, fissure at the neck.
Large beets peel naturally, small beets
are reluctant, not ripe. Greens steamed,
nubs boiled, cold garnet liquid saved
for dye, wanting this world to be
enough, I leave a taste of dirt, of earth.

— *Vivian Shipley*

Ode alla Barbabietola

Tutto ciò che devi sapere
— John Keats

Bollire le barbabietole crude per il piacere
di farlo, alla vecchia maniera, con molto lavoro,
foglie verdi increspate fischiano
a sanguinose vene. Girasoli s'affrettano
al cielo, piselli non sorretti languiscono,
ma le barbabietole sopravvivono all'ombra dei cetrioli,
piantati troppo vicini. Nello Yoga, barbabietole

non si battono per lo spazio e neppure competono
con le zucchine. I tuberi con sforzo si sollevano,
crescono, grandi o piccoli, si fendono al collo.
Le barbabietole grandi si spellano da se, le piccole
sono restie, se non mature. Le foglie cotte a vapore,
i tuberi bolliti, il rosso liquido freddo conservato
per tinture, sperando che questo mondo sia
sufficiente, lascio un sapore di sporco, di terra.

— *Vivian Shipley*
trans: *Sabine Pascarelli*

SALADS — INSALATE

Country Tuscan Bread Salad — Panzanella

Sweetcorn and Radicchio Salad — Insalata di Radicchio e Mais

Mozzarella, Tomatoes and Arrugola — Caprese con Rucola

Marinated Bean Salad with Tuna — Insalata di Fagioli e Tonno

Classic Pasta Salad — Insalata di Pasta

Ceci Bean Salad — Insalata di Ceci

Potato Salad with Seafood — Insalata di Patate e Frutti di Mare

Arrugola and Pecorino with Walnuts — Rucola e Pecorino con Noci

Cucumber Salad — Insalata di Cetrioli

Green Salad with Croutons — Insalata Verde con Croutons

Country Tuscan Bread Salad — Panzanella

8 slices stale Italian Bread
4 large ripe tomatoes
1 large red onion
2 cucumbers

1 cup red wine vinegar
Extra virgin olive oil
1 handful fresh basil
Salt and Pepper

Soak the bread in water and squeeze "dry." Dice the tomatoes, onion and cucumbers. Place in large bowl and mix well. Add basil leaves, oil, vinegar, salt and pepper. Refrigerate for one hour. Serve cold.

Sweetcorn and Radicchio Salad — Insalata di Radicchio e Mais

3 ½ oz. baby spinach
   leaves, chopped
3 radicchio, chopped
Generous ½ cup smoked
   ham, diced

Generous 1 cup canned corn,
   drained
Juice of 1 lemon, strained
Scant ½ cup olive oil
Salt

Put the spinach and radicchio in a salad bowl and add ham and corn. Put a pinch of salt in a bowl, add the lemon juice and stir to dissolve, then whisk in the olive oil. Pour dressing over salad and toss. Serves 4.

Mozzarella, Tomatoes and Arrugola — Caprese con Rucola

Alternate on a flat plate a slice of mozzarella and a slice of tomato, on a bed of arrugola. Season with salt, pepper and oregano, and drizzle with extra virgin olive oil.

Marinated Bean Salad with Tuna — Insalata di Fagioli e Tonno

16 oz. can cannellini beans, drained
(12) oz. can(s) white solid-pack tuna, drained; broken into chunks

In a large bowl, combine beans, tuna, mix gently. Combine olive oil and seasonings; mix well. Pour over gently. Cover; refrigerate at least 4 hours. Serve on a bed of lettuce with sliced black olives, and sliced hard boiled eggs as part of the mixed antipasto tray. Makes 6 servings.

Classic Pasta Salad — Insalata di Pasta

1 lb. pasta (best penne)

Boil pasta in salted water, drain and put aside until cool.

4 fresh tomatoes, chopped	Salt, pepper
2 mozzarella balls, cut into small cubes	3 t anchovies paste or anchovy filet, finely chopped
Fresh basil leaves, chopped	Chili pepper
Oregano, dry	½ cup extra virgin olive oil
Chive, chopped	

Mix the ingredients in a salad bowl, add the olive oil and seasonings. Cover and let stay in a cool place for an hour, then mix together with pasta. Accompanies meat or fish.

Pasta salad can be varied. Excellent for leftovers of vegetables, meat or fish.

Ceci Bean Salad — Insalata di Ceci

½ lb. canned ceci beans (drained)
Canned tuna in olive oil (drained)
1 leek stalk, sliced into thin rings
1 red or yellow pepper,
   finely sliced
1 garlic clove
1 onion

2 t capers
½ cup green olives
   without stones
1-2 t parsley
½ cup extra virgin olive oil
1 T white vinegar
Salt, pepper

Prepare a sauce, blending together the tuna, the finely chopped onion, capers and olives. Pour in the olive oil in a fine thread while emulsifying the ingredients to a soft cream, and pour into a small bowl.

   Now mix pepper, the leek rings and the ceci beans in a salad bowl, add the parsley and the chopped garlic, then stir in the tuna cream. Serve at room temperature. Serves 6.

Potato Salad with Seafood — Insalata di Patate e Frutti di Mare

3 cups sliced potatoes
¾ cup Italian or Greek
   sliced black olives
1 T minced parsley
¼ t basil
1 - 7 ¾ oz. can tuna fish,
   drained and cubed
1 cup cooked cleaned shrimp

3 T wine vinegar
¼ t salt
½ t freshly ground black
   pepper
1 clove garlic, minced
¾ cup olive oil
2 T anchovy paste
1 t capers

In a bowl, put the potatoes, olives, parsley and garlic. Mix together the oil, anchovy paste, capers, vinegar, salt, pepper and basil. Pour half the dressing over the vegetables and toss gently but well. Make a depression in the center, and into it pile the tuna fish. Arrange the shrimp around the edge on a bed of baby spinach or salad leaves. Pour remaining dressing over all. Serves 4-6.

Arrugola and Pecorino with Walnuts — Rucola e Pecorino con Noci

On a bed of arrugola, arrange Italian Pecorino cheese, cut into thick strips. Add chopped walnuts on top. Season with salt, drizzle with extra virgin olive oil.

Cucumber Salad — Insalata di Cetrioli

3 small cucumbers, sliced and peeled
Juice of 1 lemon, strained
1 fresh thyme sprig, chopped
1 T balsamic vinegar

2 pears
7 oz. feta cheese, diced
4 T olive oil
Salt and pepper

Blanch the cucumber slices in salted, boiling water for 3 minutes, then drain and refresh under cold water. Spread on a dish towel to dry. Peel and core the pears, then slice thinly and sprinkle with lemon juice. Make a ring of cucumber slices on each of four individual plates. Surround with ring of pear slices, then another ring of cucumber and finally, a ring of feta. Sprinkle with the thyme. Whisk together olive oil and vinegar in a bowl, season with salt and pepper and pour the dressing over the salad and serve.

Green Salad with Croutons — Insalata Verde con Croutons

Croutons
1 clove garlic, peeled and sliced
1 cup cubed stale Italian bread, with the crust removed
    (save for bread crumbs)
2 T olive oil

Salad
1 medium head iceberg or Boston lettuce
1 medium head romaine lettuce or endive
¼ cup grated Parmesan cheese

Dressing
½ cup olive oil   ½ t salt
¼ cup red wine vinegar   ¼ t pepper
½ t dried oregano, crumbled

First, prepare the croutons. Heat the olive oil in a small skillet and sauté the garlic in the oil over moderate heat until lightly browned. Remove the garlic with a slotted spoon and discard. Add the bread cubes and sauté, stirring frequently, until golden brown. Drain on paper towels.

Combine the dressing ingredients in a bottle or screw-top jar and shake well. Allow to stand at room temperature. Clean the lettuce and pat dry. Tear into bite-size pieces and place in a salad bowl. Refrigerate until serving time.

To serve, sprinkle the salad with the cheese and croutons. Shake the dressing well and pour over the salad. Toss well and serve immediately. Makes 4 to 6 servings.

Sunday

Here is a genial congregation,
well fed and rosy with health and appetite,
robust children in tow. They have come
and all the generations of them, to be fed,
their old ones too who are eligible now
for a small discount, having lived to a ripe age.
Over the heaped and steaming plates, one by one,
heads bow, eyes close; the blessings are said.

Here there is good will; here peace
on earth, among the leafy greens, among the fruits
of the gardens of the country's heartland. Here is abundance,
here is the promised
land of milk and honey, out of which
a flank of the fatted calf, thick still
on its socket and bone, rises like a benediction
over the loaves of bread and the little fishes, belly-up in butter.

— *Anne Caston*

Domenica

Qui c'è una allegra congregazione,
nutrita bene e rosea per salute ed appetito,
robusti bambini a suo seguito. Sono venuti loro
e tutte le loro generazioni, ad essere nutriti,
anche i loro vecchi che adesso sono leggibili
per un piccolo sconto, avendo vissuto fino a età matura.
Sui piatti colmi e fumanti, uno per uno,
teste si abbassano, occhi si chiudono; si dicono le benedizioni.

Qui c'è buona volontà; qui la pace
sulla terra, tra verdi foglie, tra i frutti
degli orti del cuore della campagna. Qui c'è abbondanza,
qui c'è il promesso
paese di latte e miele, dal quale
un fianco del vitello ingrassato, carnoso ancora
sul suo osso, s'innalza come una benedizione
sui pani e piccoli pesci a pancia in su nel burro.

— *Anne Caston*
trans: *Sabine Pascarelli*

Pomegranate

A geode
filled with uncut
garnets
spills onto
my plate,
seeds
never to
give birth
but gems
so radiant
and royal
I want to celebrate
the deep glory
of red,
of stones
more ardent
than burgundy,
jewels so wondrous
I want to string them
on a silken thread
twirl them round
my arms
all the way
up to my neck.

— *Alexis Rotella*

Melograno

Un geode
pieno di granati
non tagliati
cade sul
mio piatto,
semi
che mai
germoglieranno
ma gemme
così raggianti
e regali
vorrei festeggiare
l'intenso splendore
del rosso,
di pietre
più ardenti
del bordeaux,
gioielli così meravigliosi
da volerli infilare
su un filo di seta
avvolgerli intorno
alle mie braccia
tutto su
fino al collo.

— *Alexis Rotella*
trans: *Sabine Pascarelli*

Radicchio

Maybe it's the way you curl
beneath the supermarket mist,
or the ease with which you languish
beside less lovely leaves.
You call to me,
you seem to sing
a lusty song. You tempt me.

You are wound tight, ready
to be sprung, a
naughty daughter of cabbage.
A saucy Italian import, your kiss
is bitter, but you tease and glitter.

Peeling open layers,
I hate to tear and slice
such gorgeous flesh,
but you are the Alpha Romeo
of Romaine and Escarole,
the Chianti of crudités,
the Fiat of fiddleheads,
the Gucci of greenery.

Your name is like the whisper
of a starved Venetian lover
and I want you for my bed...
with a lovely scoop of tuna,
maybe sliced with lemon.

— *Christine Sostarich*

Radicchio

Forse è il modo come ti arricci
nella condensa del supermercato,
oppure l'agio con il quale languisci
accanto a foglie meno belle.
Mi chiami,
sembra che canti
una vigorosa canzone. Mi tenti.

Sei avvolta stretta, pronta
ad essere rilasciata, una
disubbidiente figlia del cavolo.
Un'impertinente importazione italiana,
il tuo bacio è amaro, stuzzichi e luccichi.

Aprendo gli strati,
mi dispiace tirare ed affettare
tale stupenda carnosità,
tu sei l'Alfa Romeo
della Romana e della Scarola,
il Chianti delle crudités,
la Fiat delle felci,
il Gucci della vegetazione.

Il tuo nome è come il sussurro
di un affamato amante veneziano
e ti voglio per il mio letto...
con una bella palettata di tonno,
affettato magari, con limone.

— *Christine Sostarich*
trans: *Sabine Pascarelli*

DESSERTS — DOLCI

Pears in Cream — Pere alla Crema

Mascarpone Tart — Tiramisú

Peaches in Red Wine — Pesche al Vino Rosso

Creamy Dessert — Zabaione

Chocolate-Wine Cake — Torta al Cioccolato con Vino Rosso

English Soup — Zuppa Inglese

Artusi's Babá — Babá dell'Artusi

Grandmother's Apple Cake — Torta di Mele della Nonna

Pato Biscuits — Cantucci di Prato

Hazelnut Cake — Torta di Nocciole

Pears in Cream — Pere alla Crema

12 firm pear halves (canned)
Light rum
6 egg yolks

6 T sugar
1 pint whipping cream

Drain pears. Marinate in ½ inch rum for 2 hours. Turn pears often. Remove pears. Reserve liquid. Place pears in serving dish. Beat egg yolks until thick. Gradually add sugar. Beat after each addition. Stir in rum to taste. Whip cream until stiff. Fold into egg mixture. Cover and chill 2 hours.

Mascarpone Tart — Tiramisú
For this recipe use Lady Fingers or sponge cake.

4 eggs, separated
8 T sugar
1 lb. mascarpone
⅛ t salt

½ lb. sponge cake (or 40 Lady
    Fingers or Pavesini)
1 cup brewed espresso
3 T cocoa powder

1. Beat the egg yolks with sugar until smooth and fluffy. Add the mascarpone and beat until well blended.
2. Using a whisk, beat the egg whites and salt until stiff peaks have formed. Fold the egg whites gently into the mascarpone/egg mixture. Set aside.
3. Dip the sponge cake in the brewed coffee and place on a plate to drain.
4. Assemble the tiramisu using the drained sponge cake as the bottom layer. Spread with mascarpone and continue layering with cake and cream until all ingredients have been used. The top layer must be cream.
5. Sprinkle with cocoa powder and refrigerate for two hours before serving.

Peaches in Red Wine — Pesche al Vino Rosso

1¼ lbs. white peaches

4 cups red wine

Scant 1 cup superfine sugar

2 T vanilla sugar

1 clove

Pinch of freshly grated nutmeg

Blanch the peaches in a pan of boiling water for 5 minutes, then drain and peel. Halve and pit them. Pour the wine into a pan, add the superfine sugar, vanilla sugar, clove and nutmeg, and simmer for 10 minutes more. Remove the peaches with a slotted spoon and place in a dish. Bring the syrup to a boil and cook until reduced and thickened. Pour over the peaches and let steep for 12 hours. Serves 4.

Creamy Dessert — Zabaione

4 egg yolks

4 T sugar

8 T Marsala

¼ t vanilla

Combine all ingredients in top of double boiler, place over hot water and beat constantly until frothy, smooth and slightly thick. Serve plain or on sponge cake, either hot or cold. Serves 4.

Chocolate-Wine Cake — Torta al Cioccolato con Vino Rosso

7 oz. butter
7 oz. sugar
3 eggs
Vanilla extract
1½ t ground cinnamon

9 oz. flour
1½ t baking powder
4 oz. red wine
3-4 T dark cocoa or grated
    semi-sweet chocolate

Cream together sugar, butter, then the eggs. Sift flour, vanilla, cinnamon, baking powder and cocoa. Mix flour mixture into butter/sugar/egg mix. Pour into buttered baking pan (with removable sides). Bake for about 45 minutes. Done when toothpick inserted in the center comes out dry.

English Soup (Rum Torte) — Zuppa Inglese

2 T cornstarch	36 Lady Fingers
½ cup sugar	1 cup rum
¼ t salt	1 cup heavy cream
2 cups milk	1 T confectioners' sugar
1 t vanilla extract	

Sift the cornstarch, salt, and sugar into a saucepan. Gradually beat in the milk, then the egg yolks. Cook over low heat, beating steadily, until thickened and smooth. Don't boil the mixture. Remove from the heat and beat in the vanilla. Strain if there are any lumps. Cool.

Line the bottom of an 11-inch, deep pie plate close with some ladyfingers; pour ¼ cup rum over it. Cover with half the cooled custard. Make another layer of ladyfingers (reserve some for the top), sprinkle with ¼ cup rum, spread remaining custard over it, and cover with remaining Lady Fingers. Sprinkle with ¼ cup rum. Cover and chill 3–4 hours. Just before serving, pour the remaining rum over the top, and cover with the cream whipped with the confectioners' sugar.

Note: Spongecake cut into Lady Finger shapes may be used in place of the Lady Fingers. Serves 8–10.

Note: A streamlined version is to buy or bake a sponge cake. Cut across in two layers. Fill each with rum. Mix French vanilla instant pudding according to directions. Pour on layers. Use remainder on top and sides. Cover with whipped cream or whip substitute.

Artusi's Babá — Babá dell'Artusi

9 oz. flour
1 pack or cubed yeast
3 oz. milk
2 oz. butter
2 oz. confectioners' sugar
2 whole eggs + 1 egg white

3 oz. raisins
1 T candied fruit
½ cup cream
½ cup marsala
½ cup rum
Vanilla extract

Melt the yeast in tepid milk, add a handful of flour and work to a small ball. Put it in a bowl, cover with a kitchen towel and let rise for ½ hour.

Cream the eggs with the sugar, add the remaining flour to smooth mixture. Add the warmed up butter, the yeast, the tepid liquid cream, marsala and rum. Work the mixture until it doesn't stick to the bowl. Add the raisins, the candied fruit, and put it back into the covered bowl for another 20 minutes to rise.

Grease a baking form with high borders with butter, spoon in the mixture, cover again with a towel, and put it aside for 2 hours in a warm place to rise. It should double its volume.

Preheat oven to 390°, put in the cake and bake until golden brown, 45-50 minutes. Let it cool out in the oven. When it is cold take it out and sprinkle with vanilla sugar.

Grandmother's Applecake — Torta di Mele della Nonna

¾ cup white sugar
5 oz. butter
3 eggs
7 oz white flour

½ t ground cinnamon
1 t baking powder
1 T rum
About 7 apples, peeled, halved,
    insides removed

Preheat oven to 350°

    Whisk sugar and butter until creamy, then whisk in eggs. Whisk in the sifted flour, cinnamon, baking powder, rum. Pour into greased baking pan (with removable sides). Arrange the apple halves on the mixture until surface is covered. Fill hollows with lingonberries, or with raisins mixed with sugar. Bake the cake for about 1 hour, until surface golden and an inserted toothpick comes out dry.

Prato Biscuits — Cantucci di Prato

7 oz. sugar
2 eggs
1 ¼ cups flour
1 T Grand Marnier

2-3 t baking powder
1 t ground aniseed
4 oz. peeled almonds

Mix the ingredients, stir in almonds at the end. Form cylinders (size of a thumb), place them without touching on a baking plate covered with baking paper, and bake them in a preheated oven at 390° for 5 minutes on each side, or until hard. (Typical of Tuscany, these are eaten at the end of a dinner, dipping them into VIN SANTO (half-sweet Tuscan wine.)

Hazelnut Cake — Torta di Nocciole
(without flour)

6 eggs
7 oz. white sugar
1 cup ground hazelnuts

For filling:
Canned cherries
Whipped cream

Preheat oven to 300°
Whip eggs and sugar with an electric beater for almost 10–15 minutes (important!), until it is very creamy, then add the ground hazelnuts.

Pour into a buttered baking pan with removable sides. Bake for about 20 minutes, until golden brown. Done when toothpick inserted in the center comes out dry. Let cool completely.

With a thin cotton thread held at the two ends, cut the cake horizontally in 2 halves. Sprinkle with red wine, drain cherries (the liquid can be heated up, stirring in the sugar and a little cornstarch to thicken it, and then added back to the cherries for the filling). Put filling on base of cake. Cover with the other half of cake. Spread whipped cream on top and all around the cake. Garnish with some cherries.

Folly

Melt one pound of butter
but do not brown.
          I saw a tranquil face
through the window of
my kitchen.

While still warm
stir in one pound of very good chocolate
and a generous pinch of salt.
          Its countenance inviting
me with epic loneliness.
Talking into icy nights
our warmed words,   retold in
daydreams of pre-defeat.

Cool.
          The hope-filled day we stood
before Leonardo's only
painting in our town,
declaring the promise

Gently stir in one-half cup of flour.
In a separate bowl,
          of knowing.

Beat eight eggs
until light and lemon colored.
          Others pondered
the painting's monetary value

Add one cup of sugar

Folly

Sciogliere mezzo chilo di burro
senza farlo imbrunire.
> *Vidi una faccia tranquilla*
attraverso la finestra della
mia cucina.

Mentre è ancora caldo
aggiungere mezzo chilo di cioccolato buono
e un buon pizzico di sale.
> *La sua espressione mi invitò*
con epica solitudine.
Parlando in notti fredde
le nostre parole riscaldate, ridette in
sogni ad occhi aperti di presconfitta.

Far raffreddare.
> *Il giorno, pieno di speranza, stavamo*
davanti all'unico quadro
di Leonardo nella nostra città,
dichiarando la promessa

Aggiungere delicatamente mezza tazza di farina.
Separatamente,
> *di sapere.*

battere otto uova
a neve leggera, color limone.
> *Altri ponderavano*
il valore materiale del quadro

Aggiungere una tazza di zucchero

and beat until thick,
   and we secreted our lone gold bounty.

like lightly whipped cream.
   I had some classic lines.

Carefully fold chocolate
mixture into
the eggs.
   I knew an ancient spice road.

The texture will change
and thicken.
   And the botanical names
of some useful plants sounding
like new poetry

Pour into ten inch round
   basilicum vulgaris-
mazus reptans

Bake for thirty mintues
at three hundred and fifty degrees
   And more than a few, good
recipes for disaster

cake should rise and crack slightly on top
   What I now know best
more comprehensively,
is the geography of shared souls.
The Brunelleschi dome of us

It will fall
   structured incomprehensibly

e montare finché avrà la consistenza
    e noi celavamo l'unico nostro dono dorato.

di una leggera panna montata
    Avevo alcune righe classiche.

Far scivolare attentamenta l'impasto
di cioccolato
nelle uova.
    Conoscevo una antica strada di spezie.

La consistenza cambierà,
addensandosi.
    Ed i nomi botanici
di alcune piante utili suonavano
come poesia nuova

Versare il tutto in uno stampo rotondo
    basilicum vulgaris-
mazus reptans-

Cuocere nel forno per trenta minuti
a centottanta gradi.
    E più che alcune buone
ricette per disastri.

Il dolce gonfierà, spaccandosi leggermente in superficie.
    Ciò che adesso so meglio,
in maniera più comprensiva,
è la geografia di anime condivise.
Noi, come il duomo di Brunelleschi,

Sgonfierà
    strutturato incomprensibilmente

in its arch
and height,
its lift and heft and weight,
like the consequences
of our inconsequentiality

and the center will remain soft.
              Now there are the smothering
distractions of our ghosts.

Cool completely.

— *Carole Wagner Greenwood*

nella sua volta
ed altezza,
il suo elevamento, portanza e peso,
come le conseguenze
della nostra inconseguenza.

e rimarrà morbido al centro.
        Adesso ci sono le soffocanti
distrazioni dei nostri fantasmi.

Raffreddare bene.

— *Carole Wagner Greenwood*
trans. *Sabine Pascarelli*

The Moments That Shine

To Maria and Mario Volpe, San Mauro, Cilento, Campania

On this clear July morning, the skin of the world is scrubbed and shining. The lemons are big yellow jewels in the trees; the grapes on the grape arbor hang in clusters so perfectly formed they could be a work of art, and I am sitting on my cousin Maria's terrace. Flowers grow all around us in plaster pots that line the walls. I feel all the taut strings of my life loosen, the air smooth as scented cream on my face,

and for one moment in these southern Italian mountains, I could almost be one of the enormous butterflies that light on the flowers and fly off, so weightless am I and happy, staring off at the mountains opposite where San Mauro, my mother's home town, is strung like a necklace across the mountain tops. Maria brings me an espresso and pastry she made just for me because I mentioned

my mother used to make it and so she got up at five a.m. to start the elaborate process and finished at 12:30, presenting me with a huge tray of *pastechelle* drizzled with honey and sprinkles and I feel welcomed in the place as though my mother and father were here with me, leading me home.

— *Maria Mazziotti Gillan*

I Momenti che Risplendono

A Maria e Mario Volpe, San Mauro, Cilento, Campania

In questa limpida mattina di luglio la superficie della terra è lavata e lucidata. I limoni sono grandi gioielli gialli negli alberi; l'uva sulla pergola pende in grappoli così perfetti da essere un'opera d'arte, ed io sono seduta sul terrazzo di mia cugina Maria. Intorno a noi crescono fiori in vasi di gesso lungo i muri. Sento allentare tutti i fili tesi della mia vita, l'aria è morbida sulla pelle come una crema profumata,

e per un momento in queste montagne del sud dell'Italia potrei anche essere una di quelle enormi farfalle che scendono sui fiori e volano via, così leggera sono, e felice, lo sguardo fisso sulle montagne di fronte, dove San Mauro, la città nativa di mia madre, è tesa come una collana intorno alle cime dei monti. Maria mi porta un espresso e dei pasticcini fatti proprio per me perché accennavo

che mia madre usava farli, così si è alzata alle cinque per preparare l'elaborato impasto e ha finito alle 12.30, presentandosi con un enorme vassoio di *pastecchelle* cosparse di miele e zucchero a velo e mi sento ben accolta in questo posto, come se mia madre e mio padre fossero qui, guidandomi a casa.

— *Maria Mazziotti Gillan*
trans: *Sabine Pascarelli*

At Babington's

In my Roman dream you meet us at the station,
your purple coat, your glasses in your hair,
and herd us all into a waiting taxi-cab, saying,
Babington's, lento, lento, grazie, in that queenly
manner nobody ignores. And Hypatia, coming forward
in the tearoom, will greet us in meticulous 5th century
Greek and escort us to a table where we will celebrate

in a glaze of damask and candelabra and a plethora
of little cakes. And you will say in your low contralto —
moonlight floating from a garden — Oh look! here comes
Mary McCarthy, arguing with Fr. Leonard Boyle on
the Procession of the Holy Ghost and *filioque*.

Everything as usual. Precisely as it should be.
Have another cake, my dear, and then we'll settle down
to serious discussion on the latest truffle find
in northern Italy, and the finest way to shred them
over salads.

— *Cicely Angleton*

Al Babington's

Nel mio sogno romano ci incontri alla stazione,
il tuo cappotto viola, occhiali nei capelli,
e ci convogli tutti al taxi che aspetta, dicendo
Babington's, lento, lento, grazie, in quella maniera
maestosa che nessuno ignora. E Hypatia, avanzando
nella sala da tè, ci saluta in un meticoloso greco del
V. secolo, per poi accompagnarci ad un tavolo, dove festeggiamo

in un bagliore di damasco e candelabri e una pletora
di dolcetti. E con la tua bassa voce di contralto dici —
il chiar di luna inondante dal giardino — guardate! Ecco
che arriva Mary McCarthy, discutendo con Fr. Leonard Boyle sulla
Processione dello Spirito Santo e *filioque*.

Tutto come sempre. Precisamente come deve essere.
Prendi un altro dolcetto, mia cara, e poi ci sistemiamo
per discutere l'ultimo ritrovamento di tartufo
nel Nord Italia, e la miglior maniera di grattarlo
sull' insalata.

— *Cicely Angleton*
trans: *Sabine Pascarelli*

IN ITALY the dust settles quickly on every floor,
be it tile or marble. It is the dust of ages and it must be
moved every day by broom and bucket and *lo straccio,*
the sturdy, wet rag moved purposefully over the floors
by a toothy mop. Women do this daily under the blank,
watchful eyes of pagan statues, or crosses, or engravings
on sacred walls and columns backed by umbrella pines,
the famous pines of Rome. It must be done to allow
the day's *allegria* to sparkle with the incandescence
of lover's greetings or the heat of ancient rancors.

Then the day can happen. The goats can go to pasture,
seeking the shade, as every automobile driver has
learned to do, following their example. Everyone
moves to the day's rhythm, the shopkeepers,
the horn blowers in cars and on motorcycles,
the gardeners in the *orti,* where vegetables swell
in the sun, waiting for cooks to handle them lovingly.
In the formal gardens, fountains splash and the eye
seeks the symmetry of hedges and sundials, the statues
changing hue as the sun moves.

                              Then comes the glow
of sunset on the warm orange *palazzi* with their
windows framed in white marble, the flags
of clothes on lines crossing the tiny byways.
The late afternoon belongs to Horace. Its light
tells of earth's bounty cultivated and savored,
the wine poured, the second nature of talk
and writing that inhabits the dust which every day
must be moved in homage.

— *Judy Neri*

IN ITALIA la polvere si deposita rapidamente su ogni pavimento,
sia mattonelle, sia marmo. È la polvere dei secoli e deve essere
rimossa ogni giorno da scopa, secchio e dallo straccio,
quel robusto, umido cencio che passa deciso sui pavimenti
sorretto da uno spazzolone dentato. Le donne lo fanno ogni giorno
sotto gli sguardi vacui di statue pagane, o croci, o incisioni
su muri sacri e colonne con lo sfondo di pini ad ombrello,
i famosi pini di Roma. Deve essere fatto per permettere
che l'allegria del giorno possa scintillare con l'incandescenza
dei saluti di amanti o col fervore di antichi rancori.

Allora il giorno si può svolgere. Le capre possono andare a
pascolare, cercando l'ombra, come ogni automobilista ha
imparato a fare, seguendo il loro esempio. Ognuno
si muove al ritmo del giorno, i bottegai,
i suonatori di clacson nelle macchine e sui motorini,
i giardinieri negli orti, dove verdure gonfiano
al sole, aspettando cuochi che sappiano maneggiarli con cura.
Nei giardini all'italiana le fontane versano e l'occhio
cerca la simmetria di siepi e meridiane, le statue
cambiano sfumatura appena il sole si muove.

                     Poi giunge il rosseggiare
del tramonto sui caldi palazzi arancioni con
finestre incorniciate di marmo bianco, bandiere
di vestiti su fili che attraversano stretti marciapiedi.
Il tardo pomeriggio appartiene ad Orazio. La sua luce
racconta della generosità della terra coltivata ed assaporata,
il vino versato, la seconda natura di linguaggio
e scrittura che abita nella polvere che ogni giorno
deve essere rimossa in omaggio.

— *Judy Neri*
trans: *Sabine Pascarelli*

Saved

I see it when I prepare food.
Chopping vegetables or pouring out grains of rice
I see how I watch the pieces that get left out
or the grains that fall away from the pot.
I always pick them up.
Taking the extra effort to wash them again
if they've landed on the floor or the counter top,
I put them back in the pan or the soup.
And always I think of the biblical story:
The gread Lord God talking
about who will live and who will die
in Sodom and Gomorrah.
Abraham asks, "If I can find fifty righteous people,
will you destroy the whole city?"
Then finally coming down to
"What about one good person—
will you destroy the whole place if I can find one good soul?"

I always think of that and save the grain of rice.
Saying this one has come so far, grown with all the others,
come finally to my kitchen, in my hand,
and now I have dropped it. So I rescue the one grain or bean.

Thinking always if someone saw me,
I would also be rescued.

When I am reminded
who I truly am—
    I am the cook.
    I am the water.
    I am the pot.
    I am the bean
    finally seen and savored.

— *Jenny D'Angelo*

Salvato

Lo vedo quando preparo il cibo.
Quando taglio le verdure o quando verso i chicchi di riso
vedo come osservo i pezzi che rimangono fuori,
i chicchi che cascano fuori dalla pentola.
Li raccolgo sempre.
Faccio lo sforzo di lavarli di nuovo
se sono finiti sul pavimento o sul piano di lavoro,
li rimetto nella padella o nella minestra.
E penso sempre alla storia biblica:
Il grande Iddio che parla
su chi vivrà e chi morirà
a Sodoma e Gomorra,
Abramo chiede, "se trovassi cinquanta persone rette,
distruggerai tutta la città?"
Per poi alla fine scendere a
"che mi dici di una persona buona—
distruggerai l'intero posto se riesco a trovare una anima buona?"

Penso sempre a questo e salvo il chicco di riso.
Dico, questo viene da così lontano, è cresciuto con tutti gli altri,
venuto infine nella mia cucina, in mano mia,
e adesso mi è cascato. Così salvo questo singolo grano o fagiolo.

Pensando sempre, se qualcuno mi vedesse,
verrei anch'io salvata.

Allorché mi ricordo
chi veramente sono—
    Sono la cuoca.
    Sono l'acqua.
    Sono la pentola.
    Sono il fagiolo
    finalmente visto e gustato.

— *Jenny D'Angelo*
trans. *Sabine Pascarelli*

FEATURED POETS

Poet and librettist **Karren LaLonde Alenier,** author of *The Steiny Road to Operadom: The Making of American Operas,* is anchored at Alenier. blogspot.com. **Barbara Goldberg** is the author of six books of poetry, most recently *The Royal Baker's Daughter* (University of Wisconsin Press, 2008), and recipient of the Felix Pollak Poetry Prize. She is senior speechwriter at AARP. **Rod Jellema** lives still in near-downtown Washington. **Rose Solari** is a poet who learned the joys of cooking from her aunt, Sarah Verdi. **Michael S. Glaser** is discovering retirement and savoring the delicious flavors of it. **Calder Lowe** is a widely-published poet, Ragdale Fellow, community outreach facilitator, former college English instructor, and Executive Editor of Dragonfly Press. **Diane Lockward,** author of *Eve's Red Dress* and *What Feeds Us* (Wind Publications), has published her poems in such journals as the *Harvard Review, Spoon River Poetry Review,* and *Prairie Schooner.* Queen of a Rainy Country is **Linda Pastan**'s latest book. She is a former Poet Laureate of Maryland and learns about cooking from her chef son. **Jean Emerson** is a poet, memoirist, and grandmother who lives in San Jose, California. **Christine Sostarich** is a freelance writer and poet who lives in the Pocono mountains of Pennsylvania with her four children and husband to whom she dedicates the poem that appears in this book. **David Budbill** lives in the mountains of northern Vermont where he gardens and cuts firewood. **Moira Egan** lives, writes, and cooks in Rome. **Judy Neri** has lived in Italy and speaks and cooks in Italian whenever possible. **Anne Caston** is the author of two collections of poetry: *Flying Out With The Wounded* (1997) and *Judah's Lion* (2009). **Alexis Rotella**, a prominent figure in the world haiku community, lived in Northern Italy for three years. **Cicely Angleton** lives in Great Falls and is author of *A Cave of Overwhelming: Selected Poems* (with Eugenia Schultheis) and *Inventory* (with Reed Whittemore and Elaine Magarrell). **Patricia Gray** believes poetry and food are necessary for life. She is the author of *Rupture: Poems.* **Ernie**

Wormwood is in Leonardtown, Maryland eating oysters and loving longer. **Christina Daub** is having a plum time teaching poetry at George Washington University. **Maria Mazziotti Gillan**, founder and director of the Poetry Center at Passaic County Community College in Paterson, New Jersey, and director of the Creative Writing Program at Binghamton University—SUNY, received the American Book Award for her latest book, *All That Lies Between Us* (Guernica Editions). **Jenny D'Angelo** lives in the coastal town of Santa Cruz, where many marvelous things, including her four chickens, the gathering shorebirds, and the shining sea become the ingredients for poems. **Vivian Shipley** says, "cooking beets makes me feel like I'm a girl again going out to the vegetable garden on my Grandma and Grandpa Shipley's farm in Hardin County, Kentucky." **Carly Sachs** is a writer, yogini, and foodie living in Brooklyn, New York. **Nan Fry**, author of *Relearning the Dark*, teaches at The Writer's Center in Bethesda, Maryland. **Katherine J. Williams**, Associate Professor Emeritus at George Washington University, is a psychologist and art therapist who practices in the Washington, DC area. **Carole Wagner Greenwood** is a James Beard Award nominated Chef (Buck's Fishing & Camping, Comet Ping Pong) and a plaster sculptural artist, represented by Civilian Art Projects, all in Washington, DC. **Andrea Hollander Budy**, the author of three poetry collections, is the Writer-in-Residence at Lyon College in Batesville, Arkansas. **Emily Ferrara** is author of *The Alchemy of Grief* (2007), winner of the Bordighera Poetry Prize. Ms. Ferrara's favorite childhood meal was Nonni's spaghetti and tomato sauce with *bracciole*.

ACKNOWLEDGMENTS

"Saved" appeared in *Harvest from the Emerald Orchard* published by Emerald Street Press, Santa Cruz, CA, 2007. "Pomegranate," *Camembert Comes From The Sea*, White Peony Press, 1984. "Cynara scolymus" [Artichoke] from the manuscript *Strange Botany*. "Folly" by permission of the author Carole Wagner Greenwood. "Tomatoes in September" *Happy Life: new poems*, by David Budbill, Copper Canyon Press. "Linguini," *What Feeds Us*, Wind Publications, 2006. "The Moments That Shine," *Ocho 12, Goss183: Casa Menendez* and *What We Pass On: Collected Poems*, Toronto, Canada, Guernica Editions, 2009. "Sunday Brunch," *Flying Out With The Wounded*, New York University Press, 1997. "Pears," *Setting the Table*, Dryad Press, 1980. "In Italy The Dust," *Always the Trains*, Scarith Books, New Academia Publishing, 2008. "In My Sister's Garden," *Rupture*, Red Hen Press, 2005. "Onions," *Innisfree Poetry Journal* 6 (March 2008). "Soup," *House Without A Dreamer*, Story Line Press, 1993. "The Gourmand's Prayer," *The Royal Baker's Daughter*, University of Wisconsin Press, 2008. "Green Beans," *A Slender Grace*, William B. Eerdmans Publishing Co., 2005.

THE CHEFS

Grace Cavalieri has written several books of poetry and 21 produced plays. Among production awards, "Quilting the Sun" received a key to the city of Greenville, South Carolina, at its 2007 premiere. Her book of poems, *Water on the Sun,* was listed on Pen American Center's "best books list," and won the Bordighera Poetry Prize in 2005. Her latest collection is *Anna Nicole: Poems* (2008), which received the 2009 Paterson Award for Literary Excellence. Cavalieri founded "The Poet and the Poem" on public radio now celebrating its 33rd year on the air. She now produces the series "From the Library of Congress." She lives in Maryland with her sculptor husband Ken Flynn. They have four daughters and four grandchildren.

Sabine Pascarelli is the Italian translator of *Alchemy of Grief* that won the Bordighera Poetry Prize in 2006. She grew up in Germany where she earned a degree in literature at Dortmund University. She is an author of children's literature. Her most recent book, published in Germany, is *Glenscheck & Co.* She has won fiction awards, from La Spezia, Italy, and most recent, Mirabilia, in 2006. Recent poems were in the English journals *Only the Sea Keeps* and *Arabesque.* She works as a translator of English, Italian, and German. Pascarelli lives in Tuscany with her husband Salvatore and their two sons, Marco and Claudio. She is a visual artist as well as a poet.

VIA FOLIOS
A refereed book series dedicated to Italian studies and the culture
of Italian Americans in North America.

Most Recent Titles

EMANUEL DI PASQUALE
Siciliana
Vol. 60, Poetry, $8.00

NATALIA COSTA-ZALESSOW, ED.
Autobiographical Poems
Vol. 59, Poetry, $18.00

RICHARD VETERE
Baroque
Vol. 58, Fiction, $18.00

LEWIS TURCO
La Famiglia/The Family
Vol. 57, Poetry, $12.00

NICK JAMES MILETI
The Unscrupulous
Vol. 56, Humanities, $20.00

PAOLINO ACCOLLA &
NICCOLÒ D'AQUINO
Italici:
An Encounter w/ Bassetti
Vol. 55, Italian Studies, $8.00

GIOSE RIMANELLI
The Three-Legged One
Vol. 54, Fiction, $15.00

CHARLES KLOPP, ED.
Bele Antiche Stòrie
Vol. 53, Italian Cultural Studies, $25.00

JOSEPH RICAPITO
Second Wave
Vol. 52, Poetry, $12.00

Other VIA FOLIOS Titles

ADKINS, ET.AL, BRENT: *Shifting Borders*; Vol. 42, Cultural Criticism, $18.00
ANGELUCCI, GIANFRANCO: *Federico F.*; Vol. 50, Fiction, $16.00
BAROLINI, HELEN: *Chiaroscuro: Essays of Identity*; Vol. 11, Essays, $15.00
BAROLINI, HELEN: *More Italian Hours & Other Stories*; Vol. 28, Fiction, $16.00
BELLUSCIO, STEVEN: *Constructing a Bibliography*; Vol. 37, Italian Americana, $15.00
BRIZIO-SKOV, ED., FLAVIA: *Reconstructing Societies in the Aftermath of War*; Vol. 34,
      History/Cultural Studies, $30.00
CANNISTRARO, PHILIP: *Blackshirts*; Vol. 17, History, $12.00
CARNEVALI, EMANUEL W/ DENNIS BARONE, ED. & AFTERWORD: *Furnished Rooms*; Vol. 43, Poetry,
      $14.00
CASEY, ET. AL, JOHN: *Imagining Humanity*; Vol. 25, Interdisciplinary Studies, $18.00
CLEMENTS, ARTHUR L. *The Book of Madness and Love*; Vol. 26, Poetry, $10.00
CONDINI, NED: *Quartettsatz*; Vol. 7, Poetry, $7.00
CORSI, JONE GAILLARD: *Il libretto d'autore, 1860–1930*; Vol. 12, Criticism, $17.00
DEVRIES, RACHEL GUIDO: *Teeny Tiny Tino*; Vol. 47, Children's Literature, $6.00
DIPASQUALE, EMANUEL: *Writing Anew,* Vol. 46, Poetry, $15.00
FAMÀ, MARIA: *Looking for Cover*, Vol. 45, Poetry, $15.00; CD, $6.00

FEINSTEIN, WILEY: *Humility's Deceit: Calvino Reading Ariosto Reading Calvino*; Vol. 3, Criticism, $10.00

GARDAPHÈ, FRED L. *Moustache Pete is Dead!* Vol. 13, Oral literature, $10.00

GARDAPHÉ, FRED, PAOLO GIORDANO, AND ANTHONY JULIAN TAMBURRI: *Introducing Italian Americana: Generalities on Literature and Film*; Vol. 40, Criticism $10.00

GIORDANO, ED., PAOLO A. *Joseph Tusiani: Poet, Translator, Humanist*; Vol. 2, Criticism, $25.00

GIOSEFFI, DANIELA: *Blood Autumn / Autunno di sangue*; Vol. 39, Poetry, $15.00/$25.00

GIOSEFFI, DANIELA: *Going On*; Vol. 23, Poetry, $10.00

GIOSEFFI, DANIELA: *Word Wounds and Water Flowers*; Vol. 4, Poetry, $8.00

GRAMSCI, ANTONIO; TRANS. AND INTROD. BY PAOLO VERDICCHIO: *The Southern Question*; Vol. 5, Social Criticism, $5.00

GUIDA, GEORGE: *Low Italian*; Vol. 41, Poetry, $11.00

HOSTERT, ANNA CAMAITI, and ANTHONY JULIAN TAMBURRI, EDS. *Screening Ethnicity*; Vol. 30, Ital. Amer. Culture, $25.00

LAGIER, JENNIFER: *Second Class Citizen*; Vol. 19, Poetry, $8.00

LIMA, ROBERT: *Sardinia • Sardegna*; Vol. 24, Poetry, $10.00

MESSINA, ED., ELIZABETH GIOVANNA: *In Our Own Voices*; Vol. 32, Italian American Studies, $25.00

MISURELLA, FRED: *Lies to Live by*; Vol. 38, Stories, $15.00

MISURELLA, FRED: *Short Time*; Vol. 8, Novella, $7.00

MORMINI, GARY: *Italians in Florida*; Vol. 51, History, $15.00

NASI, ED., FRANCO: *Intorno alla Via Emilia*; Vol. 27, Culture, $16.00

PARATI, GABRIELLA, and BEN LAWTON, EDS. *Italian Cultural Studies*; Vol. 29, Essays, $18.00

PASQUALE, EMANUEL DI: *The Silver Lake Love Poems*; Vol. 21, Poetry, $7.00

PICARAZZI, TERESA, and WILEY FEINSTEIN, EDS. *An African Harlequin in Milan*; Vol. 10, Theater/Essays, $15.00

PUGLIESE, STANISLAO G. *Desperate Inscriptions*; Vol. 31, History, $12.00

RICAPITO, JOSEPH: *Florentine Streets and Other Poems*; Vol. 9, Poetry, $9.00

RUSTICHELLI, ED., LUIGI: *Seminario sul racconto*; Vol. 16, Narrativa, $10.00

RUSTICHELLI, ED., LUIGI: *Seminario sulla drammaturgia*; Vol. 14, Theater/Essays, $10.00

STEFANILE, FELIX: *The Country of Absence*; Vol. 18, Poetry, $9.00

TALARICO, ROSS: *The Journey Home*; Vol. 22, Poetry, $12.00

TALARICO, ROSS: *The Reptilian Interludes*; Vol. 48, Poetry, $15.00

TAMBURRI, ED. ET. AL., ANTHONY JULIAN *Italian Cultural Studies 2001*; Vol. 33, Essays, $18.00

TAMBURRI, ED., ANTHONY JULIAN with MARY JO BONA, INTROD. *Fuori: Essays by Italian/American Lesbians and Gay*; Vol. 6, Essays, $10.00

TAMBURRI, ED., ANTHONY JULIAN: *Italian Cultural Studies 2002*; Vol. 36, Essays, $18.00

TURCO, LEWIS: *Shaking the Family Tree*; Vol. 15, Poetry, $9.00

TUSIANI, BEA: *con amore*; Vol. 35, Memoir, $19.00

TUSIANI, JOSEPH: *Ethnicity*; Vol. 20, Selected Poetry, $12.00

VALERIO, ANTHONY: *Tony Cade Bambara's One Sicilian Night*; Vol. 44, Memoir, $10.00

VALERIO, ANTHONY: *The Little Sailor*; Vol. 49, Memoir, $9.00

VISCUSI, ROBERT: *Oration Upon the Most Recent Death of Christopher Columbus*; Vol. 1, Poetry, $3.00

Published by BORDIGHERA, INC., an independently owned not-for-profit scholarly organization that has no legal affiliation to the University of Central Florida or John D. Calandra Italian American Institute, Queens College/CUNY.

Breinigsville, PA USA
10 November 2009
227359BV00001B/7/P